For my exceptional siblings,
Maria, Niki and Bambos

By the same author

Angels of Morphia

We've Got Simple, We've Got Complicated

Sirens of the Tundra

A collection of articles published in the *Parikiaki* and the *Hellenic Post* newspapers

---

James Neophytou

Sirens of the Tundra

Author: James Neophytou

First Published in 2025

ISBN 978-1-83538-604-0 (Paperback)

Book cover design and Book layout by:
Maple Publishers
www.maplepublishers.com

Published by:
Maple Publishers
Fairbourne Drive, Atterbury,
Milton Keynes,
MK10 9RG, UK
www.maplepublishers.com

A CIP catalogue record for this title is available from the British Library.

‘**Neo:** Why do my eyes hurt?
Morpheus: You’ve never used them before.’

— *The Matrix* (1999)

‘If you’re not sure what to do with the ball, just pop it in the net, and we’ll discuss your options afterwards.’

— Bill Shankly

Contents

Introduction

A Jewish man and a Chinese man were conversing.

The Jewish man commented upon what a wise people the Chinese are.

'Yes,' replied the Chinese man, 'our culture is over four thousand years old. But you Jews are also a very wise people, too.'

The Jewish man replied, 'Yes, our culture is over five thousand years old'.

The Chinese man was incredulous. 'That's impossible,' he replied. 'Where did your people eat for a thousand years?'

This book is a collection of articles that were originally published in the *Parikiaki* and the *Hellenic Post* newspapers, and on *Substack*.

London

March, 2025

I – Women

'Πυρ, γυνή και θάλασσα, δυνατά τρία'

'Fire, woman and the sea – the mighty three.'

– Aesop

1 Simone III

Simone and the Ancients

Simone Weil, the French philosopher and political activist, deserves wider recognition. She had a deep appreciation for the Ancient Greeks and their works. She delved into the works of Homer, Sophocles, and Plato, among others.

Simone Weil's influential book '*Intimations of Christianity among the Ancient Greeks*' revolves around the belief that certain concepts and themes present in Ancient Greek thought and literature foreshadowed or resonated with the Christian ideas and values that came after. She further explores these parallels in her book '*Gravity and Grace*' and in various essays.

Weil argues that the Ancient Greeks had glimpses or intuitions of truths that would later find their full expression in Christianity. She believed that despite the absence of a direct knowledge of Christ, the Greeks possessed a longing for divine truth and exhibited qualities that could be seen as precursors to Christian virtues.

One key aspect of Weil's idea is the concept of '*metachi*,' which she borrows from Plato's dialogue '*Phaedrus*.' *Metachi* refers to the intermediate spaces or intermediaries that bridge the gap between the visible and invisible, the material and spiritual realms. Weil saw *metachi* as a manifestation of the Christian concept of the Incarnation, where the divine and the human are united. She believed that the Ancient Greeks, through their myths, rituals, and art, sought to express and explore these intermediary realms.

For example, in her essay '*The Love of God and Affliction*,' Weil suggests that the Greek myths of *Eros* and *Psyche* offer glimpses of divine love and the human soul's quest for union with the divine. She finds in these myths echoes of the Christian understanding of God's love for humanity and the yearning for communion with God.

Weil also emphasises the Greek concept of '*kenosis*', or self-emptying, as a parallel to the Christian idea of self-sacrifice. In her essay '*Forms of the Implicit Love of God*,' she writes, 'The Greek spirit was the first to grasp the intellectual meaning of the Christian *kenosis*.' She points to the works of Aeschylus, where heroes willingly undergo suffering and self-sacrifice for the greater good, as a precursor to the Christian notion of Christ's sacrifice on the cross. Prometheus is invoked as a Christ 'type', being hung up high to suffer for helping humanity. Icarus as the fallen angel.

Weil draws attention to the Greek idea of '*logos*', meaning both reason and *word*, which she sees as an anticipation of the Christian notion of *the Word* made flesh in Christ. She highlights Heraclitus and the Gospel of John's prologue as examples of this parallel.

Weil fuses the influences on Christianity by the Ancient Greeks, and finds a resonance that points to a deeper spiritual and human truth. Her exploration of these intuitions of Christianity among the Ancient Greeks serves to bridge the gap between the two traditions and highlight the universality of spiritual ideas.

In her brilliant essay '*The Iliad, or the Poem of Force*', Weil provides a profound analysis of Homer's epic. She explores the theme of force and its impact on humanity, drawing attention to the destructive nature of violence. Weil's quote, 'Force is as pitiless to the man who possesses it, or thinks he does, as it is to its victims; the second it crushes, the first it intoxicates,' reveals her profound understanding of the dynamics of power and its consequences, which resonates with Homer's classic depiction of the Trojan War.

Regarding Sophocles, Weil wrote extensively on his play '*Antigone*' and its exploration of moral conflict. She highlights Antigone's rebellion against an unjust law and the clash between human and divine laws. Weil's quote, 'The true hero, the true subject at the centre is force,' demonstrates her ability to grasp the underlying themes and philosophical questions posed by Sophocles.

14th September 2023

2 Camille

Gender warfare and the old country ways

Camille Paglia, Professor of Humanities, University of Philadelphia, in conversation with Jordan Peterson, Professor of Psychology, University of Toronto, 2017.

Paglia: We are witnessing the decline of Western culture. Masculinity still exists in the world, but only as a code among Jihadists. We have passionate masculinity circling the borders, like the Huns and Vandals during the Roman empire.

Young women today are unhappy. Wherever I go, anywhere in the world - Italy, Brazil, England, America, Toronto - upper middle class professional women are miserable. They don't know why, and they blame it on men.

I have an idea of why we're having these problems. I come from an immigrant family. When I was young, I remember the life of the agrarian era, which accounts for most of human history. There was the world of men, and the world of women. The sexes had very little to do with each other. Each had power and status in its own realm. And they laughed at each other.

Women had enormous power. Especially the old women, who had status and ruled, not like today. The older you were the more control you had over everyone: mating, marriage, childbirth, inherited knowledge.

I remember the joy women had with each other, all day long - cooking, companionship, talking. My mother remembered as a child in Italy, taking the laundry up the hill to the fountain - la sorgente - and doing it by hand. They would sing and picnic. We glimpse that in *The Odyssey* when Odysseus is shipwrecked on Phaeacia. He hears young women laughing and singing. It's the princess, Nausicaa, bringing the women to do the laundry.

Each gender had its own hierarchy, values, and way of talking. The sexes rarely intersected.

I remember in childhood, during the holidays - Christmas or Thanksgiving - the women would be cooking all day, everyone would sit down to eat, and after that the women would retire en masse to the kitchen. I would look through the window, and see all the men outside, gathered around the car. The hood would be up and the men would be standing with their hands on their hips staring at the engine. That's how I learned that men refreshed themselves by studying something technical and mechanical, after being with the women during the dinner.

Never in human history have men and women worked side by side.

Today's problems are the result of women's emancipation from housework thanks to capitalism, which made it possible for women to have jobs outside the home - no longer dependent on husband, father, or brother.

This great thing that happened to us, allowing us to be self-supporting, independent agents, has also produced this animosity between men and women.

Peterson: Three things separate women and men, psychometrically.

Firstly, *agreeableness*: women are on the whole more agreeable – interpersonal closeness, compassion, politeness, and a desire to avoid conflict.

Second, women are higher in *negative emotion:* anxiety and emotional pain.

Third is their *interests*: women are interested in people, and men are interested in things. That goes nicely with your car anecdote.

Paglia: My father could never follow women's conversations. Women don't finish sentences; they understand immediately what the other woman is saying.

Soap operas accurately mirror the way women talk. These communication patterns were built up over centuries. Division of labour made sense. *It wasn't sexism.* The men went off to hunt, doing the dangerous things. Women stayed around the hearth. The hunting parties of Native Americans would last for weeks. Many died when the temperatures were below zero.

The answer, is *education*, into *early history*.

12th October 2023

3 Parthenogenesis

'Then said Mary unto the angel, 'How shall this be, seeing I know not a man?''

— Luke 1: 34

The late Archbishop Desmond Tutu used to tell a joke about Mary, heavily pregnant, and Joseph, looking for a place to stay in Bethlehem. Joseph rushes up to the innkeeper.

Joseph: *Oh please. Please help me, please help me. My wife is about to have a baby.*

Innkeeper: *Sorry, it's not my fault.*

Joseph: *It's not mine either.*

A small subset of animals can have offspring without mating. The process, called parthenogenesis, allows creatures from honey bees to rattlesnakes to have so-called 'virgin births.'

Such events can shock those who care for the animals. Examples include a zebra shark named Leonie, at *Australia's*

Reef HQ Aquarium, who stunned her keepers in 2016 when three of her eggs hatched into living pups.

A few years earlier, at *Louisville Zoo*, a python named Thelma – who had never even seen a male python – laid six eggs that developed into healthy young snakes. In 2006, at *Chester Zoo*, a Komodo dragon named Flora achieved a similar feat, puzzling keepers.

Parthenogenesis comes from two Greek roots that translate to 'virgin creation.'

Reproduction involves an egg cell and a sperm cell each providing half the genetic information needed for a living organism. In parthenogenesis, the body finds a way of filling in for the genes usually provided by sperm.

Ovaries produce eggs through a process called meiosis, where the cells replicate, reorganise, and separate. These eggs contain only half the mother's chromosomes, with one copy of each chromosome.

The process of meiosis also creates a by-product: smaller cells called polar bodies, distinct from the fertile egg. In one version of parthenogenesis called automixis, an animal can merge a polar body with an egg to produce offspring. This process, which has been documented in sharks, slightly shuffles the mother's genes to create offspring that are similar to the mother but are not exact clones.

In another form of parthenogenesis, apomixis, reproductive cells replicate via mitosis, a process in which the cell duplicates to create two cells – a kind of genetic copy-and-paste. Offspring produced this way are genetically identical to the parent. This form of parthenogenesis is more common in plants.

For most organisms that reproduce through automixis, the offspring typically gain two X chromosomes from their mother, giving rise to only female offspring.

For millions of years animals have reproduced through parthenogenesis, which first emerged in some of the smallest, simplest organisms. For more advanced animals like vertebrates, scientists think that the ability to reproduce asexually came about as a last-ditch effort for species facing adverse conditions. That may explain why parthenogenesis is possible in desert and island species.

The ability to reproduce asexually allows animals to pass on their genes without spending energy finding a mate, and so can help sustain a species in challenging conditions. If a Komodo dragon arrives on an uninhabited island, for example, she alone could create a population through parthenogenesis. Because every individual would be genetically identical, Komodo dragon mothers and their daughters would be more vulnerable to disease and environmental changes than a genetically-varied group.

In areas of New Mexico, some populations of female whiptail lizards share nearly-identical genetic profiles.

Parthenogenesis occurs in more than 80 vertebrate species, half of which are fish or lizards.

2nd May 2024

4 Moneypenny

'Miss Moneypenny, forget the usual repartee, 007 is in a hurry.'

— M

Name: Moneypenny. Her first name is never specified in the James Bond films. In some of Ian Fleming's original Bond books, she is called Jane.

Occupation: Secretary to M, Head of the *Double-O* section at MI6.

MI6: The UK's Secret Intelligence Service work secretly around the world to make the UK safer. For over 100 years SIS has ensured the UK and its allies keep one step ahead of adversaries. They are highly creative, using cutting-edge technology and espionage.

Origin: Miss Moneypenny was originally inspired by Kathleen Pettigrew, secretary to the longtime head of MI6 Stewart Menzies. Additional inspirations include other intelligence secretaries, and women with whom Fleming had had romantic trysts. Fleming was himself a lieutenant commander in the British Navy.

Character Traits: Intelligent, witty, loyal, and competent. Moneypenny often engages in playful banter with secret agent James Bond, but is also deeply professional and highly efficient in her role.

Repartee: A quick and witty exchange of remarks between people. It's characterized by sharp, clever, and humorous responses and counter-responses, often showcasing the speakers' wit and verbal dexterity.

Relationship: James Bond and Miss Moneypenny have a notorious and unique relationship in the Bond series, characterised by: -

1. *Playful banter:* Their interactions are often filled with flirtatious and humorous exchanges. Bond teases Moneypenny, and she responds with witty retorts, creating a light-hearted and charming dynamic.
2. *Unspoken attraction:* There is an undercurrent of mutual attraction and affection between them. However, it remains largely unspoken and unfulfilled, adding an element of tension and charm to their relationship.
    - Bond: *'What can I bring you back from Istanbul, Moneypenny?'*
    - Moneypenny: *'A diamond. In a ring.'*
3. *Professional respect:* Despite the playful nature of their interactions, there is a strong sense of professional respect between Bond and Moneypenny. Moneypenny is loyal and competent in her role, and Bond appreciates and respects her contributions.
4. *Loyalty:* Moneypenny is a reliable and supportive figure for Bond. She often provides assistance and information crucial to his missions, and she is someone Bond can trust within the bureaucratic environment of MI6.

They each slightly envy the other. Bond sees in Moneypenny the trappings of desk bound safety, the lure of hum-drum regularity, and the temptations of domesticity. Whereas Moneypenny imagines Bond's cunning adventures of danger, and in exotic climates with mysterious and alluring people - friends and foes alike.

Miss Moneypenny's romantic life is never fully explored in the films or novels.

Workplace Romances

A 2018 survey by *Totaljobs,* showed that 22% of UK workers have dated a colleague. Another survey by *Reboot Digital Marketing* found that nearly 40% of UK workers had experienced a workplace romance.

Workplace romances in the UK are neither uniformly disastrous nor universally successful. They can lead to happy relationships or they cause personal and professional complications. The data highlights a significant portion of successful outcomes, balanced by notable risks and negative fallout.

Moneypenny serves as a stable and reliable foundational ballast to Bond's life in the *field of operations,* or *combat theatre.* She attests to Bond's dual nature as both a lethal agent and a romantic figure. As Bond accumulates body counts, Moneypenny is the gamekeeper and recordkeeper.

Bond's 'body count'

Across 25 films, 007's total *kill count* comes in at 411 - an average of 16 per film. In the 14 books, the average kill count is ten per book. Bond's reputation for seduction is as notable as his license to kill. The count of his sexual encounters numbers 58 in the films, around 2 per film. The same as in the books.

Miss Moneypenny is an essential and beloved character in the James Bond franchise, known for her sharp wit, unwavering loyalty, and the special bond she shares with James Bond. While her personal life, including romantic interests, remains in the background, her presence adds depth and continuity to the series.

28th August 2024

II – Men

'I ain't got no problem with them folks in Vietnam.
*No Viet Cong ever called me n****r.'*

– Muhammad Ali, 1967

'The Trojans never did any harm to me.'

– Achilles, 750 BCE

5 Winston

Smelling the coffee with Winston Churchill

'To defend a country, you need an army, but to defend an identity, you need a school'.

— The late Chief Rabbi, Lord Sacks

In the 1930s, Winston Churchill was the first - and often the only - voice to sound the alarm on Adolf Hitler. He was ignored pretty much throughout the 1930s, up until Hitler started invading European countries. The final trigger was Poland.

How was this? Why is it that he was the key person to spot the rising Nazi virus. What was this special alchemy about him, that allowed him to register the tremors before anyone else?

The answer, according to historian Andrew Roberts, is threefold. Firstly, he was a philosemite. Second, he was a historian. And lastly, he had seen true, fanatical fundamentalism up close.

Philosemite

Churchill liked Jews. He had grown up with them, his father had liked them, he had been on holiday with them and he recognised the contribution that Jews had made to Judaeo-Christian civilisation. Jews make up 0.2% of the world's population and yet have won 22% of all the Nobel Prizes - excelling in the fields of physics, economics, music, art, mathematics, chemistry, politics, and literature.

He was a supporter of the creation of the state of Israel, as originated in the Balfour Declaration in 1917. He had an early warning system about Hitler and the Nazis, that was not bestowed upon many of the other upper class English people of his age and generation, many of whom were antisemitic.

Standing by Jews as the forefront of civilisation. We need to heed this message; especially today.

Historian

Churchill was able to place the threat of Nazi Germany in the context of the long continuum of British history. The threat of the Spanish Armada of 1588; the threat of Louis XIV at the time of the wars of Spanish succession, which Churchill's own ancestor John Churchill, the Duke of Marlborough, was instrumental in defeating; the threat of Napoleon; and then the First World War in which he himself had fought in the trenches.

So he was able to see these four great threats in history, and he slipped Hitler into the position of the 'fifth great threat'. A threat significantly greater than any of the previous four.

Fundamentalism

Lastly, he knew what fanaticism was, as he had experienced it. Churchill had persuaded the *Daily Telegraph* to take him on, aged 23, as a war correspondent. In 1897, he travelled to the North West frontier of India and Pakistan to join the Malakand Field Force fighting against the Afghan tribes. Then he had fought in Sudan. So he had seen Islamic fundamentalism and he recognised the same tropes, the same essence, the same motifs in the Nazis - the hatred of democracy, the ability to turn reality on its head.

The other Prime Ministers of the 1930s - Neville Chamberlain, Ramsay Macdonald, Stanley Baldwin - had never seen fanatics before in their lives at all. Churchill was able to spot this special thing about the Nazis, and to warn, and warn, and warn.

Just because people didn't listen to him, he didn't change his message. Many politicians today will change their message depending on the opinion polls, or what current social media engagement and trends were saying.

The conveyor belt of today's career politicians - school, university, internship, activism, and then an elected seat - means that they haven't had such worldly experiences, and haven't walked in other people's shoes.

Churchill didn't listen to opinion polls or what the newspaper editorials were saying. He said what he believed and he carried on saying it, until he was proved right.

7th August 2024

6 Honour

Honour among Generals

From 'The Last of the Mohicans', by James Fenimore Cooper (book) / Michael Mann (film)

A battlefield in the Americas. French and English forces stand to attention facing each other. Their commanders begin a parley. The year is 1757.*

French commander General Louis-Joseph Montcalm, the Marquis of Saint-Véran, sweeps his plumed hat in an elaborate, courtly bow. British Colonel Edmund Munro briefly bows his head, more curtly than courtly.

MONTCALM: Colonel Munro, I have known you as a gallant antagonist. I am happy to make your acquaintance as a friend.

MUNRO: And I yours, Monsieur le Marquis.

MONTCALM: Please accept my compliments for the strong and skilful defence of your fortress. Under the command of a lesser man it would have fallen long ago.

MUNRO: Monsieur le Marquis, I'm a soldier, not a diplomat. You called this parley for a better reason than an exchange of compliments.

MONTCALM: You have already done everything which is necessary for the honour of your Prince. But now, I beg you to listen to the admonitions of humanity. I beg you to consider my terms for your surrender.

MUNRO: Perhaps the General's glass can reach to the Hudson and can see the size and imminence of the army of Webb?

Montcalm appears genuinely sympathetic to Munro.

MONTCALM (quietly): My scouts intercepted this dispatch intended for you.

Munro is suspicious.

French Captain BOUGAINVILLE reads the dispatch.

BOUGAINVILLE: 'Colonel Munro, at Fort William Henry. I have no men available to send to your rescue. It's quite impossible. I advise you to seek terms for surrender. I remain, General Webb, at Fort Edward.'

Munro is rocked, as if struck by a blow. Bougainville hands the letter to English Major Heyward.

HEYWARD: (*confirming*) This is the signature of Webb. (*To Munro*) And I know the temper of our men. Rather than spend the war in a French prison in Hudson Bay, they'd fight to the end.

MUNRO: You have heard your answer, Monsieur le Marquis. (*Salutes*).

Munro starts off. Montcalm stops him.

MONTCALM: Sir. I am incapable of mistreating brave men. I beg you not to sign the death warrant of so many until you have listened to what I have to say.

MUNRO: Go on ...

MONTCALM: None of your men will see the inside of a prison barge. They're free to go, so long as they return to England and fight no more on this continent, and the civilian militia return to their farms.

MUNRO: Their arms?

MONTCALM: They may leave the fortress fully armed.

Munro is impressed with Montcalm's generosity.

MUNRO: The honours of war?

MONTCALM: Granted.

MUNRO: My colours?

MONTCALM: Carry them to England, with pride.

MUNRO: Allow me to consult with my officers.

As he turns, something has broken inside Munro that can never get put back together. He speaks with his captains.

MUNRO: I have lived to see things I never expected. A British officer afraid to support another. And a Frenchman too honest to profit by that advantage. Death and honour are thought to be the same. Today, I have learned that sometimes they are not.

Munro turns toward Montcalm. Their eyes meet across the scarred battlefield.

MUNRO: Monsieur le Marquis, I am deeply touched by such unusual and unexpected generosity. My fort is yours – under the condition that I be given until dawn to bury my dead, to prepare my men and women for the long journey ahead, and turn my wounded over to your surgeons.

MONTCALM: Granted, Monsieur.

Montcalm bows deeply.

The English prepare to leave for England.

---

* - Parley *(from French: parler, 'to speak')*: a discussion between enemies. Attacking an enemy during a parley is considered a gross breach of the rules of war.

23rd May 2024

7 Varoufakis

Greek Minister of Awesome

An evening with Yanis Varoufakis, at The Prince Charles Cinema – 13th February 2024

Yanis Varoufakis, Professor of Economics, has lived at the coalface of running a country. In 2015, he was asked by Greece's President Alexis Tsipras to leave his academic career to become Greece's Minister of Finance during the years of financial crisis and European bailouts.

He became notorious for his uncompromising negotiating style against German Chancellor Angela Merkel. A reputation helped by the fact that he was usually the smartest person in the room. The Managing Director of the *International Monetary Fund*, Christine Lagarde, famously said, 'Of course, Yanis, you are right. But we have no choice. We must impose austerity on Greece.'

He is now a regular on the international speaking circuit – I've gone to see him twice in London – and a darling of the Left.

Varoufakis has coined a catchy term for his take on modern capitalism: '*Technofeudalism*'. It's the name of his latest book.

It's a compelling description: with our modern, technology overlords charging us rents for their platforms. They're not interested in profits anymore, as they make so much from this platform rent. (Leave your phone at home for 2 hours, and then check your anxiety levels. It's a life support machine.)

Varoufakis has since started his own political party, called *Democracy in Europe 2025 (DiEM25)*. But, he's been unable to generate much support in his own country – managing just 3% of the vote in the last Greek General Election. So now he seeks a wider coalition across a dozen countries, under the *DiEM25* banner. A new 'Internationalist' movement.

The world is not that interested, it's fair to say. He is an entertainer, not a political leader.

The tide of trade

Fifty years ago, the world had 9 out of 10 people living in extreme poverty. '*Extreme Poverty*' is defined by the *United Nations* as 'living on less than $2 a day'. Today, the world has less than 1 person in 10 living in extreme poverty.

This has come about through free trade, open markets, global investments, capital mobility, labour mobility, education, less regulation, fewer price controls, more enterprise, the profit motive and lower protectionism in markets. The exact opposite of *Varoufakis-ism,* in fact. There has been no 'Poverty Tsar' orchestrating events.

Corbyn appears

I went along to a screening of a new Varoufakis documentary called '*In the Eye of the Storm: The Political Odyssey of Yanis Varoufakis*', hoping to learn something new.

It was the same old story, told by Varoufakis over six episodes. Thankfully, only two were screened.

When the screening was over, the audience asked Yanis some questions.

And then, in the dark, draughty depths of the auditorium, someone stood up like a shadowy Emperor Palpatine, and raised his hand. He had no question. Just an incoherent ramble about separating economics from politics, and wanting to 'take control away from the sophistry of the moneylenders'.

'*Moneylenders*'. We all knew who he meant. He just couldn't help himself.

It was Jeremy Corbyn. The crowd was delighted. I cringed. Or winced. Whichever you prefer. I think I prefer cringed.

Corbyn has spent 41 years as an MP. Almost half a century. There is no record of a Corbyn Private Member's Bill, no memorable Corbyn question, not a single speech in a debate, no record of any presence on a Standing Committee or Select Committee. He has doubtless served his constituents. Fine. But he's spent his entire career talking to people who already agree with him.

Yanis finished the evening saying, 'I'm actually very popular with Greek Orthodox monks. They're always coming up to me. We seem to have a lot in common – believing in something just for the sheer hell of it.'

11th July 2024

8 Assange

Guilty as charged. Free as a bird

Wikileaks founder Julian Assange has walked free from a US court after pleading guilty in a deal to end a 14 year-long legal battle.

Assange was pursued by US prosecutors for leaking a vast amount of secret military information, and had faced the risk of a long prison sentence.

He is now a judicially proven convicted criminal. He spent five years in London's Belmarsh prison, and before that he spent seven years hiding from justice, in the Ecuadorean embassy.

Narcissism

There is a terrific long-form essay in the *London Review of Books* by Andrew O'Hagan in March 2014, that profiles the über-hacker.

O'Hagan had been commissioned to ghost write Assange's autobiography – a project which never materialised because of Assange's bizarre eccentricities and unreliability. The essay recounts O'Hagan's experiences in trying to make it work.

He stays with Assange and his entourage. He attends meetings, eats with him, and describes a tortuous few months when day was night, and light was dark.

It's a masterly study of modern narcissism and ideological confusion. Assange is a walking contradiction.

More harm than good

Assange has a polarising effect on people. There is no doubt that he has created increased national security risks. His release of classified information via *WikiLeaks* exposed sensitive intelligence and military operations, potentially endangering the lives of informants, military personnel, and civilians.

These leaks strained diplomatic relations between the US and other countries, as confidential diplomatic communications were made public, leading to mistrust and tension.

Assange started his journalistic career as a hacker. He developed the dark art of 'cyber-espionage', and has encouraged its proliferation, leading to increased incidents of cyber-attacks and data breaches.

Diplomats and politicians cite his undermining of democratic processes. The release of hacked emails during the 2016 US presidential election has been one of the factors argued to have influenced the outcome.

What he does is illegal. Assange's methods and motivations have been questioned, with accusations that he selectively released information to serve specific political agendas, raising ethical concerns about his objectivity and transparency.

More good than harm

To play devil's advocate, Assange's work with *WikiLeaks* has exposed government misconduct, corruption, and human rights abuses, perhaps promoting greater accountability. By releasing classified documents, Assange has championed the principle of freedom of information, arguing that citizens have a right to know what their governments are doing.

Assange's profile and activism has provided a means for other whistle-blowers to safely disclose information, shedding light on issues that might otherwise remain hidden. Most prominently Bradley (now Chelsea) Manning and Edward Snowden. Snowden now lives in hiding in Russia, as a fugitive from justice.

The leaks have informed the public about significant global issues, sparking debates and leading to policy changes and reforms.

Assange has challenged the concentration of power and secrecy in governments and corporations, advocating for greater democratic oversight and civil liberties.

Legacy

The evaluation of Julian Assange's impact is disputed. Supporters argue that he has promoted public awareness by exposing government misconduct and advocating for freedom of information.

Critics contend that his actions have endangered lives, strained diplomatic relations, and undermined democratic processes, raising significant legal and ethical concerns.

Ultimately, the assessment hinges on the balance between the right to know and the potential harms caused by the distribution of classified or sensitive information.

One legacy remains. A long line of discarded colleagues and betrayed fellow travellers who showed loyalty to Assange, but to whom no loyalty was shown by him.

Failing to sentence Assange could set a precedent that undermines the legal accountability for unauthorised publication of classified materials, and may cause more harm than good.

4th July 2024

9 Aristotle

The king's teacher: Alexander and Aristotle

'Ω παι, ζήτει σεαυτώ βασιλείαν ίσην. Μακεδονία γαρ σε ου χωρεί'
'My son, seek out a kingdom equal to thyself; Macedonia cannot contain you.'

— King Philip II, of Macedonia

The philosopher Aristotle tutored Alexander the Great for about seven years, from 343 BCE to 336 BCE, starting when Alexander was around 13 years old.

King Philip II of Macedon, Alexander's father, brought Aristotle to the Macedonian court to educate his son in a wide range of subjects, including philosophy, ethics, science, politics, and the arts. They studied in Miesa, a secluded place near Pella, to provide Alexander with a peaceful environment for learning.

Lessons

Aristotle emphasised the importance of self-discipline, logical reasoning, and the pursuit of knowledge. He instilled in Alexander an admiration for Homer's works, especially the *Iliad,* which became one of Alexander's lifelong inspirations. Aristotle even gifted Alexander an annotated copy of the *Iliad,* which the young prince reportedly kept under his pillow during his campaigns. The set of scrolls was '*corrected by Aristotle*', according to one of Alexander's officers, Onesicritus, who wrote a (now lost) history of his commander.

Aristotle also introduced Alexander to the concept of *natural law* – that there is an order and logic to the universe – and encouraged him to apply this reasoning to governance and warfare. The tutor often stressed the balance between reason and ambition, warning Alexander not to let his desire for conquest overpower his moral compass.

Adventures

Bucephalus: One famous story during Aristotle's time as Alexander's tutor involves Bucephalus, the wild horse. When the horse refused to be tamed, Aristotle allegedly encouraged Alexander to observe carefully. Alexander noticed the horse was afraid of its own shadow and managed to calm and tame it. While Aristotle didn't directly handle the horse, his emphasis on observation and reasoning likely influenced Alexander's approach. It was on seeing Alexander tame the horse that his father Philip encouraged his son to seek new kingdoms.

Defiant Student: Despite their close relationship, Alexander's fiery nature sometimes clashed with Aristotle's calm philosophy. Alexander once questioned the practical value of some of the more abstract philosophical teachings, asking, 'How will this help me in battle?' Aristotle quipped back that while tactics win battles, wisdom wins wars.

Alexander's response to criticism: Aristotle was known for his critiques of monarchy as a form of governance, preferring rule by a virtuous elite. Alexander, destined to be a monarch, playfully retorted, 'And yet, teacher, here you are, educating a future king!'

Curiosity: When Alexander later began his conquests, he sent back samples of flora, fauna, and cultural artifacts to Aristotle. One report suggests Alexander once sent Aristotle a live crocodile, along with a note saying, 'I found something even logic might struggle to explain!'

Legacy

The relationship between Aristotle and Alexander was significant because it laid the intellectual foundation for Alexander's future as a conqueror. Aristotle's teachings didn't just shape Alexander as a warrior but also as a ruler who valued culture and knowledge. Alexander's efforts to spread Greek ideas and language across his empire – the so-called Hellenisation – can be directly tied to his tutor's influence.

Although their relationship cooled in later years – perhaps because of Alexander's increasing obsession with his own divinity and his absolute rule – Aristotle's teachings remained a cornerstone of Alexander's worldview. The blend of reason and ambition that Aristotle cultivated helped Alexander change the world, even as he stretched beyond the boundaries of what his teacher might have envisioned.

Aristotle's influence

Aristotle's influence extends far beyond his own time, impacting various fields of knowledge and shaping the intellectual traditions of Western civilisation. His work laid the foundation for many disciplines: -

Theophrastus: Aristotle's most prominent student and his successor at the Lyceum, Theophrastus continued Aristotle's work in botany, biology, and ethics.

Medieval Islamic scholars: Thinkers like Avicenna (Ibn Sina) and Averroes (Ibn Rushd) preserved, expanded, and transmitted Aristotle's works, influencing medieval Europe. Arabic scholars were among the first translators of Aristotle, and it is possible we would not know his work, were it not for them.

Christian theology: Thomas Aquinas integrated Aristotelian logic and metaphysics into Christian theology, shaping the Scholastic tradition. Aristotle plays a central role in Dante's epic *The Divine Comedy.*

The Enlightenment: His emphasis on empirical observation influenced later scientific methodology and thinkers like Francis Bacon and Galileo.

Modern science and philosophy: Fields such as biology, ethics, political science, and logic owe a debt to Aristotle's systematic approach and foundational ideas.

Alexander's influence

Alexander's legacy is monumental, particularly in terms of the cultural, political, and military impacts of his conquests.

By founding cities like Alexandria in Egypt, Alexander spread Greek culture, language, and ideas across the vast territories he conquered, from the Mediterranean to the Indus River. This cultural blending created the Hellenistic Era.

Alexandria became a major centre of learning and culture, housing the famous Library and fostering advancements in science, mathematics, and philosophy.

After his death, Alexander's empire split into the Hellenistic kingdoms (e.g., Ptolemaic Egypt, Seleucid Empire), each carrying forward his legacy of Greek governance blended with local traditions.

Later rulers, from the Roman Caesars to Napoleon, admired and emulated Alexander's military strategies and vision for empire-building.

The spread of Greek '*Koine*' language became the accepted common tongue of the Hellenistic world, which significantly influenced early Christianity and the dissemination of the New Testament.

Alexander's innovative phalanx formations and cavalry strategies inspired generals throughout history, including Hannibal, Caesar, and Frederick the Great.

For later generations, Alexander's story inspired countless leaders, artists, and writers. His campaigns are celebrated in works like Plutarch's *Parallel Lives* and Arrian's *Anabasis of Alexander*.

Alexander became a symbol of ambition, courage, and the human drive to achieve greatness, even to the point of hubris.

Together, Aristotle and Alexander, shaped the ancient world and continue to resonate through history, each in their own monumental way.

4th January 2025

10 Aristotle II

The Italian and Arabic influence

Aristotle's influence is deeply embedded in Dante Alighieri's works, particularly in *The Divine Comedy*.

Dante revered Aristotle as 'the master of those who know,' reflecting the widespread respect for Aristotle in medieval Europe as the cornerstone of intellectual thought. Here are the key traces of Aristotle in Dante's work.

Ethics

Dante's moral and ethical vision in *The Divine Comedy* is heavily influenced by Aristotle's *Nicomachean Ethics*.

Using the 'threefold division of sins', in the *Inferno*, Dante adopts Aristotle's classification of sins as found in *Ethics* and *Rhetoric*, namely - incontinence: Sins arising from lack of self-control, such as lust, gluttony, and greed; violence: Sins involving harm to others, oneself, or nature; and fraud: The most grievous sin, involving deliberate deception and betrayal. This structure shapes the hierarchical organisation of *Hell* in Dante's vision.

Dante incorporates Aristotle's idea that human happiness comes from pursuing the 'highest good,' which Aristotle defines as a life of virtue and intellectual contemplation. Dante Christianises this concept, framing the beatific vision of God as the ultimate fulfilment of human purpose.

Dante frequently refers to Aristotle simply as '*The Philosopher*,' reflecting his status as the preeminent authority on human reason. In *Inferno* (Canto 4), Aristotle is placed in the first circle of Hell, or Limbo, among virtuous pagans who lived before Christ. Dante reverently describes him as sitting at the centre of a group of wise men, including Plato and Socrates, signifying his role as the intellectual cornerstone of ancient thought.

Dante incorporates Aristotle's teachings on persuasion, particularly the use of ethos (character), pathos (emotion), and logos (reason), to guide his narrative style.

Arabic

It is highly possible that much of Aristotle's work would have been lost to history had it not been for the efforts of Arabic translators and scholars during the Islamic Golden Age (8th–13th centuries).

After the fall of the Western Roman Empire in the 5th century CE, much of the knowledge of ancient Greek philosophy, including Aristotle's works, became inaccessible in Europe.

The Latin-speaking West had limited access to Aristotle, primarily through partial works or summaries written by Roman authors like Cicero and Boethius.

Many of Aristotle's original Greek texts were lost or forgotten in Europe during the Early Middle Ages.

Aristotle's works were preserved in the Byzantine Empire and transmitted to the Arab-speaking world through translations into Syriac by Christian scholars, such as those in the Nestorian tradition.

Then, scholars such as Hunayn ibn Ishaq (9th century) and his school played a critical role in translating Aristotle's works from Greek into Arabic. They also added their own commentaries to clarify and contextualise the texts. Hunayn translated works like *De Anima* and *Physics*. Thābit ibn Qurra and other scholars refined translations to make them more faithful to the original Greek texts.

Islamic philosophers like Al-Kindi, Al-Farabi, Avicenna (Ibn Sina), and Averroes (Ibn Rushd) not only preserved Aristotle's texts but also expanded on them, integrating Aristotelian thought with Islamic theology and making significant advancements in philosophy, science, and medicine.

Transmission

During the 12th century, Aristotle's works returned to Europe through the efforts of translators in places like Spain (particularly in Toledo) and Sicily.

In the 13th century, there was a resurgence of interest in Aristotle's original Greek texts, facilitated by Byzantine scholars. However, by then, the Arabic translations had already played a critical role in preserving his works and stimulating European intellectual life.

The Arabic scholars and translators were pivotal in preserving Aristotle's legacy during a time when his works were largely inaccessible in Europe. They not only safeguarded his writings but enriched them with interpretations that influenced both the Islamic and Western intellectual traditions. Without their efforts, our understanding of Aristotle today might be significantly diminished.

4th January 2025

III – Health

'Whatever you do, always give 100%.

Unless you're donating blood.'

—Bill Murray

11 Green

'Once I saw the river clean.'
- Morrissey

In 1983, a commercial fishing company bought a patrol boat to monitor the Hudson river, in New York state. They began suing over 500 polluters, forcing them to spend $5bn on the environmental remediation of the Hudson.

The river would catch fire from the flammable paint waste from *General Motors* car factories. The river would turn whatever colour they were using that week to the paint the trucks in Tarrytown. It was dead water - zero dissolved oxygen for twenty miles north of New York City, twenty miles south of Albany - no life in it.

Today, the company is a registered social enterprise known as *Riverkeepers*, and as a result of their work, the Hudson is now the richest waterway in the north Atlantic. It produces more biomass per gallon, more pounds of fish per acre than any other waterway in the Atlantic ocean, north of the Equator.

It's now an international model for ecosystem protection. The Hudson is now the only waterway on the north Atlantic that still has strong spawning stocks of all of its historical species of migratory fish - striped bass, sturgeon, herring and blue crab.

Riverkeepers' mission is 'to protect the environmental, recreational and commercial integrity of the Hudson River, and safeguard the drinking water of nine million New York residents.'

The miraculous resurrection of the Hudson inspired the creation of new *Riverkeepers,* making it the biggest water protection group in the world, with 350 waterkeepers inspecting their local waterways. They sue polluters in 46 countries.

In 2005, *Riverkeepers* across the USA and Canada sued coal-burning power plants and cement kilns for discharging mercury. The *US National Academy of Sciences* and the *Food and Drugs Administration* (FDA) agency published a report, after a five year study, which showed that every fresh water fish in America had dangerous levels of mercury in its flesh.

The commercial fishermen also declared that goldfish were dying in Walkill Creek, a western tributary of the Hudson. A new sewer plant was discharging chlorine. It's very difficult to kill goldfish; it's one of the hardiest species in the world - you can pour oil on a goldfish and nothing will happen to it. The *Department of Environmental Conservation* denied that there even *were* any goldfish in the Hudson river. But scientists changed their minds when presented with new evidence, and by listening to ordinary people with valid experience.

Institutional collusion

Regulatory capture occurs when independent agencies, which are meant to serve the public interest by overseeing industries and enforcing regulations, instead become influenced by the corporations they're supposed to regulate.

This can happen for many reasons, including the close relationship between regulators and the industries, the revolving door phenomenon (regulators moving between government and industry positions), and the asymmetry of information between the regulators and the regulated.

This happens in Financial Services. Powerful financial institutions exert significant influence over regulatory bodies, and this leads to lax oversight, inadequate enforcement, and policies that downgrade consumer interests. It also happened in the pharmaceutical industry with lobbying, campaign contributions, and cosy relationships. This resulted in unsound drug approvals and suspect pricing practices.

When government agencies are toothless and lack capability, the industry declines even further - this is known in economics as 'government failure'.

In the UK, the period between 2010 and 2021 is known as the era of *austerity*. The budgets of government bodies such as the *Environment Agency* were cut drastically. They were not able to function effectively. This is apparent in the relative ease with which the water companies were able to pour sewage into England's rivers and the sea.

7th September 2023

12 Weed

The State of New York legalised the sale of cannabis in 2022. Marijuana shops are now everywhere in the midtown and downtown districts of the city.

Like the repeal of alcohol prohibition in 1933, this recent legalisation aims to redirect the flow of monies away from criminal profits and into official private enterprise, and the subsequent tax into the revenue of each State and to the Federal government.

Let's play Avvocato del Diavolo

A number of advantages are put forward by the proponents of legalisation.

Economic boost: Legalising cannabis can create new industries, and stimulate economic growth, as seen in the states that have already made the move, like Colorado and California.

Criminal justice reform: Legalisation can reduce arrests and incarceration rates for low-level cannabis offenses, addressing the issues of documented socio-economic disparities in arrests.

Regulation and safety: Legalisation allows for better quality control, product testing, and formal and proper labelling, ensuring consumers have access to safer products.

Medical benefits: Cannabis has demonstrated medical potential, and legalisation can improve access for patients seeking relief from various conditions like back pain, rheumatism, arthritis, asthma, migraines and sleep disorders.

Consumer choice: Legalisation respects individual freedom and the right to make choices about personal consumption.

Law enforcement focus: Police resources can be redirected toward more serious crimes, enhancing overall public safety.

Reduced shadow market: Legalisation can eliminate illegal markets, minimising criminal activity associated with the drug trade.

Tourism and hospitality: Cannabis tourism can attract visitors, boosting the hospitality sector and local economies.

Harm reduction: With proper education and regulation, legalisation can lead to more responsible use and harm reduction, with visible awareness campaigns covering the risks.

Research opportunities: There may be an accelerated opportunity to deepen scientific understanding into the potential benefits and risks of cannabis use.

And the reasons against legalising cannabis

Public health concerns: Cannabis use may lead to physical and mental health issues, including addiction, impaired cognitive function, and increased risk of paranoia.

Gateway drug: Some worry that cannabis use could lead to the use of more potent, harmful, unregulated and illegal substances.

Driving safety: Legalisation may lead to an increase in impaired driving incidents, posing risks to road safety.

Youth access: Wider and prominent availability makes it easier for minors to access cannabis, impacting their health and development.

Workplace productivity: Cannabis use could affect workplace productivity and safety, particularly in jobs that require alertness and precision.

Unknown long-term effects: We. Just. Don't. Know. Enough. More research is needed to fully understand the long-term effects of cannabis use, especially with higher potency products.

Environmental impact: Cannabis cultivation has an environmental footprint, including water usage, sub-optimal land cultivation and energy consumption.

Mental health: Long term marijuana use has been linked to an increased risk of anxiety, depression, and psychosis. The conditions that it purports to help.

Regulatory challenges: Establishing and enforcing regulations for cannabis is complex and resource intensive.

Stigma and societal impact: Some opponents argue that cannabis legalisation could normalise drug use and have broader negative impacts on society.

Facts and trials

Worldwide there have been radical drug programmes that have succeeded.

Portugal decriminalised the possession of small quantities of all drugs in 2001. Instead of prosecuting drug users, they are referred to a dissuasion commission for treatment. This has reduced drug-related deaths to below the European average.

Under Switzerland's heroin-assisted treatment programme, users receive prescribed heroin with medical supervision, this has improved health outcomes and reduced crime.

Now that it's the law, perhaps New York State can use its new tax revenues to invest in combatting NYC's homelessness problem, and avoid the disastrous tent cities of San Francisco and Los Angeles.

23rd November 2023

13 Tigers

Tips from apex felines

Energy conservation is not just a principle for environmental sustainability but also a vital aspect of human efficiency and personal well-being.

Just as various animals exhibit remarkable strategies to conserve energy, humans can also learn to minimise energy wastage in daily life.

By conserving energy, individuals can channel their efforts towards meaningful and productive tasks. Reducing unnecessary energy expenditure can lead to better physical and mental health. Efficient energy use contributes to a more sustainable lifestyle, reducing one's environmental footprint.

Animals

Bears enter a state of hibernation during winter, significantly lowering their metabolic rate to survive months without eating. During hibernation, a bear's heart rate drops from 40 - 50 beats per minute to 8 - 19 beats per minute. Periodic rest and downtime are crucial. Humans should also schedule regular breaks to recharge.

Hummingbirds enter a state of torpor, a short-term hibernation, to conserve energy during cold nights or food scarcity. This can reduce a hummingbird's energy expenditure by up to 95%.

Camels have adapted to conserve energy and water in harsh desert climates by walking slowly and efficiently. Camels can effectively travel up to 100 miles without water.

Tigers

Tigers are apex predators, meaning that they're at the top of the food chain, without natural predators of their own. They are renowned for their strength and efficiency. They exhibit fascinating energy conservation behaviour in how they allocate time for rest, hunting, and enjoying their prey.

Tigers sleep or rest for an average of 16 - 20 hours per day. This extensive rest period allows them to conserve energy for hunting and other vital activities. They often sleep in shaded areas during the day to stay cool and become more active during dawn and dusk, which are prime hunting times.

Tigers typically hunt for 2 - 4 hours per day. They are solitary hunters, relying on stealth and power to catch their prey. Given their need to conserve energy, tigers usually hunt large prey such as deer, wild boar, and buffalo, which can provide a substantial amount of food from a single kill. On average, a tiger is successful in about 1-in-10 to 1-in-20 hunts. This means they must be strategic and efficient to ensure a successful kill.

Once a tiger has made a kill, it spends a significant amount of time consuming its prey. A single large kill can provide several days' worth of food. Tigers can consume up to 40 kg (88 lbs) of meat in one sitting. They then rest and digest their meal, maximising energy absorption. After a kill, tigers often drag their prey to a secluded spot to eat undisturbed. They may also cover the remains to protect it from scavengers and return to feed later.

Lessons for us: a guide for the perplexed

Prioritise: Focus on high-impact tasks that align with your long-term goals. Use techniques like the *Eisenhower Matrix* to categorise tasks by urgency (x-axis, Low to High) and importance (y-axis, Low to High).

Social interactions: Limit engagement in trivial disputes and conversations. Prioritise communication effort to manage time and energy spent on social interactions.

Mental energy: Practice mindfulness and meditation to reduce mental fatigue. Avoid multitasking, as this leads to decreased productivity and increased cognitive load.

Rest: Like tigers, ensure you get ample rest and sleep. Quality sleep is crucial for maintaining high energy levels and overall health. Schedule regular breaks throughout the day to recharge.

Avoid trivialities: Focus effort on yielding the highest return for your effort, similar to how tigers hunt larger prey for greater energy payoff. Avoid overextending yourself with too many low-impact activities.

1st June 2024

14 5k

Anatomy of a 5km run

A five kilometre run involves several biological, physiological, mental, and cardiovascular events.

Biological and physiological

1. Musculoskeletal system

Muscle contraction: The leg muscles, including hamstrings, calves, quadriceps, and glutes, engage in repetitive contractions to sustain running. Depending on the individual's muscle mass and strength, muscle fibres work hard to maintain the pace.

Joints: The knee and ankle joints, which bear the brunt of the impact, undergo stress. Over time, cartilage may wear down, making joint movement less smooth. The synovial fluid in the joints provides lubrication.

Bone density: Running imposes load-bearing stress on bones, which can help maintain bone density.

2. Cardiovascular system

Heart rate: As you run, your heart rate increases to pump more blood and oxygen to the working muscles. The maximum heart rate is calculated as 220 minus your age.

Blood flow: The heart pumps more blood with each beat - increased stroke volume - enhancing the delivery of oxygen to muscles.

Blood pressure: Systolic blood pressure (the pressure in the arteries when the heart contracts) may rise during the run, but with regular exercise, resting blood pressure can improve over time. The body redistributes blood away from organs that are non-essential at the time of running - like the digestive system - to the muscles.

3. Respiratory system

Breathing rate: The respiratory rate increases to meet the higher oxygen demands. The lungs work harder to oxygenate the blood and expel carbon dioxide.

Oxygen utilisation: As you run, the body's cells require more oxygen. The efficiency of oxygen exchange in the lungs determines how hard the body has to work to get the necessary oxygen.

4. Metabolism and energy use

Glycogen stores: The body relies on glycogen (the body's stored form of sugar) in the muscles and liver for energy. During a 5k, glycogen is broken down into glucose, which is then used by the muscles. Efficient use of glycogen stores determines whether or not you feel any fatigue.

Fat metabolism: As glycogen stores deplete, the body increasingly relies on fat as an energy source, especially during a slower-paced 5k.

Lactic acid: Lactic acid may build up in the muscles as a by-product of anaerobic respiration, especially if there's insufficient oxygen supply.

Mental and psychological impact

Endurance: Running for anywhere between 20 and 50 minutes requires sustained mental focus and perseverance.

Endorphin release: Exercise stimulates the release of endorphins, the body's natural painkillers and mood elevators, which leads to a 'runner's high' and improves mood and mental wellbeing.

Stress reduction: Running reduces levels of cortisol, the stress hormone, contributing to overall relaxation and well-being.

Recovery

Hydration: After running, it's crucial to rehydrate to replace fluids lost through sweat. Moderate use of electrolyte rich drinks can restore sodium, potassium, and other essential minerals.

Nutrition: Consuming a balanced meal, or protein-rich snack, and carbohydrates post-run replenishes glycogen stores and repairs muscle tissue. Protein is vital for muscle recovery.

Rest: Adequate rest is essential to allow muscles and joints to recover. This includes sleep (7 - 8 hours a night). A walk on the following day promotes blood flow and reduces stiffness.

Muscle soreness: Delayed onset muscle soreness (DOMS) requires gentle stretching, foam rolling, or light massage to alleviate discomfort.

Frequency

Regularity: Running a 5k two to three times a week at a moderate pace is generally safe and beneficial for maintaining cardiovascular health, muscle tone, and overall fitness.

Cross training: Incorporating other forms of low impact exercise, like swimming, on non-running days can enhance overall fitness.

Maintaining this routine can contribute to cardiovascular health, weight management, and mental wellbeing, providing a strong foundation for healthy ageing.

1st June 2025

15 Sleep

Good sleeping habits: Adding five years to life

Women who have high quality sleep have a greater life expectancy of 2.4 years, according to a US study, while for men it was even more beneficial at 4.7 years.

Research based on more than 170,000 people living in the US found those who had five healthy sleep factors were less likely to die prematurely.

They were sleeping between seven and eight hours a night, having difficulty falling asleep no more than twice a week, trouble staying asleep no more than twice a week, not using any sleep medication, and feeling well rested after waking up at least five days a week.

'If people have all these ideal sleep behaviours, they are more likely to live longer,' said Dr Frank Qian, Clinical Fellow in Medicine at the *Harvard Medical School* and co-author of the study. 'So, if we can improve sleep overall, and identifying sleep disorders is especially important, we may be able to prevent some of this premature mortality.'

He suggested that people should start trying to optimise their sleeping habits 'from a young age', adding: 'If people can develop these good sleeping habits of getting enough sleep, making sure they are sleeping without too many distractions and have good sleep hygiene overall, it can greatly benefit their overall long-term health.'

'It's important for younger people to understand that a lot of health behaviours are cumulative over time. We like to say, 'It's never too late to exercise or stop smoking,' it's also never too early. And we should be talking about and assessing sleep more often.'

The study's results are being presented at the *American College of Cardiology's* Annual Scientific Session, along with the *World Congress of Cardiology.*

The team analysed data from 172,321 people aged 50 on average, taking part in a national survey between 2013 and 2018.

They were followed up for an average of just over four years, during which time 8,681 people died, including 2,610 deaths from cardiovascular disease and 2,052 from cancer. The researchers concluded that 8 per cent of the deaths could be attributed to poor sleep patterns.

After taking into account other factors known to boost the risk of premature death, such as previously diagnosed medical conditions and alcohol consumption, people who had all five healthy sleep factors were 30 per cent less likely to die than those who had none or only one.

They were 21 per cent less likely to die from cardiovascular disease specifically, and 19 per cent less likely to die from cancer.

'We saw a clear dose-response relationship, so the more beneficial factors someone has in terms of having higher quality of sleep, they also have a stepwise lowering of all cause and cardiovascular mortality,' said Qian.

'I think these findings emphasise that just getting enough hours of sleep isn't sufficient. You really have to have restful sleep and not have much trouble falling and staying asleep.'

The researchers said their study was limited by the fact that habits were self-reported. But it fits with earlier research linking poor sleep with heart problems, and linking the disorder sleep apnoea with conditions including high blood pressure, atrial fibrillation and heart attacks.

A separate study presented at the same conference found that salt intake can be too low for heart failure patients.

Researchers analysed nine randomised controlled trials into sodium intake, and found that reducing it below the recommended maximum of 2.3g per day did not bring additional benefits, and could actually increase the risk of death.

Dr Anirudh Palicherla of *Creighton University School of Medicine* in Omaha, Nebraska, the study's lead author, said: 'Restricting dietary sodium to less than the usual recommendation was counterproductive in the management of heart failure.'

The NHS says adults should consume no more than 6g of salt a day, about one teaspoon, which contains 2.4g of sodium.

11th January 2025

16 Pose

Power and confidence

Amy Cuddy is a social psychologist best known for her research on non-verbal behaviour, power dynamics, and the effects of body language on self-confidence and performance.

Her work on 'power posing' became popular after her 2012 *TED Talk, Your Body Language Shapes Who You Are*. It is one of the most-viewed *TED Talks* of all time.

Contribution

1. Power posing

Cuddy's research, conducted with Dana Carney and Andy Yap, suggested that adopting 'high-power poses' (e.g., standing tall with arms outstretched, or with arms on hips, like Wonder Woman) could increase testosterone, decrease cortisol (the stress hormone), and make individuals feel more confident and assertive.

She argued that 'power posing' could lead to improved performance in high-stakes situations, such as job interviews or public speaking, even if practiced for just two minutes beforehand.

2. Imposter syndrome

In her 2015 book *Presence: Bringing Your Boldest Self to Your Biggest Challenges,* Cuddy explored how small changes in body language and mindset could help people overcome imposter syndrome and perform more authentically.

She emphasises 'personal power' over 'power over others,' advocating for practices that help individuals feel grounded and confident.

3. Nonverbal communication

Cuddy's broader research explores how nonverbal cues (like posture and facial expressions) influence not only how others perceive us, but also how we perceive ourselves.

Controversy

After the initial publication of her findings, Cuddy's research on power posing came under significant scrutiny during the 'replication crisis' in psychology, a movement that has revealed that many psychological studies cannot be replicated with consistent results. Cuddy faced three challenges.

1. Failed replications

In 2015, Dana Carney, one of Cuddy's co-authors, publicly distanced herself from the power posing research, stating that the effects on hormones were not replicable and that she no longer stood by the claims.

Independent replication studies have consistently failed to find evidence that power poses significantly affect testosterone, cortisol, or behaviour in the way Cuddy's original study suggested.

2. Criticism

Critics argued that the original study's sample size was too small and that statistical methods may have inflated the significance of the findings.

Some accused Cuddy of overstating the practical applications of power posing, particularly in her public appearances.

3. Backlash

The backlash became personal, with Cuddy facing intense criticism, including public shaming and online harassment. Some academics accused her of overhyping unproven science to gain fame and commercial success.

The controversy sparked a broader debate about the ethics of science communication and the role of public figures in popularising academic findings.

Verdict

The consensus among scientists today is that the original claims about hormonal changes (testosterone and cortisol) have not been reliably replicated and are considered unsubstantiated.

While the hormonal effects remain doubtful, some evidence suggests that adopting expansive postures can improve subjective feelings of confidence and reduce perceived stress. These effects are likely psychological rather than physiological.

Cuddy continues to advocate for 'power posing' as a tool for improving confidence, albeit with a more cautious framing. She now emphasises the subjective benefits (how you feel) rather than biological effects.

Conclusion

Despite the controversy, Cuddy remains a respected figure in popular psychology for her contributions to discussions on nonverbal behaviour and presence.

Cuddy's work on body language has sparked both inspiration and intense debate. While the claims about power posing's physiological effects have largely been debunked, the idea that body language can influence confidence and self-perception remains influential.

Her experience also highlights the challenges of translating academic research into popular culture and the risks of oversimplification in science communication.

29th January 2025

IV – Culture

'When the data and the anecdotes disagree, the anecdotes are usually right.'

– Jeff Bezos

17 Turkish

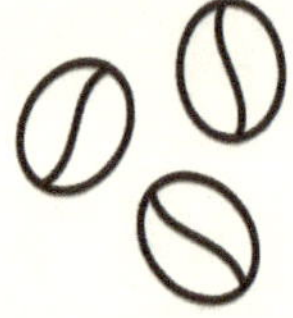

A record of a meeting at the U.N. to discuss Turkish Coffee

The *United Nations Educational, Social, and Cultural Organisation (UNESCO)* - Representative List of the Intangible Cultural Heritage of Humanity.

Decision of the Intergovernmental Committee: 8.COM 8.28

The committee: takes note that Turkey has nominated Turkish coffee culture and tradition (No. 00645) for inscription on the *List of Intangible Cultural Heritage.*

Turkish coffee combines special preparation and brewing techniques with a rich communal traditional culture.

The freshly roasted beans are ground to a fine powder; then the ground coffee, cold water (and if required, sugar) are added to a coffee pot called a *tzezve* and brewed slowly on a stove to produce the desired foam, and to a create a strong, aromatic brew.

The beverage is served in small cups, accompanied by a glass of water, and is mainly drunk in coffee-houses where people meet to talk, share news, read newspapers and books, and plot revolutions.

The tradition itself is a symbol of hospitality, friendship, refinement and entertainment that permeates all walks of life. An invitation for coffee among friends provides an opportunity for intimate talk and the sharing of daily concerns.

Turkish coffee also plays an important role on social occasions such as engagement ceremonies and holidays. The knowledge and rituals around its preparation are transmitted informally by family members through observation and participation.

The grounds left in the empty cup are often used to tell a person's fortune - this practice is called *fal*.

Turkish coffee is regarded as part of Turkish cultural heritage: it is celebrated in literature and songs, and is an indispensable part of ceremonial occasions.

The committee: decides that the nomination satisfies the following criteria for inscription on the List:

1: Passed on from generation to generation within Turkish families, the knowledge and skills related to the tradition of Turkish coffee provide a sense of identity and continuity, reinforcing social cohesion and openness through hospitality and entertainment.

2: Inscription of Turkish coffee culture and tradition on the Representative List could promote greater visibility of the intangible cultural heritage and provide an example of a social institution favouring dialogue.

3: On-going and proposed safeguarding measures demonstrate the commitment of the local and national authorities as well as of coffee aficionados and associations to promote Turkish coffee culture.

4: Several community members, experts, and associations participated in preparing the nomination, and gave their free, prior, and informed consent.

The committee hereby inscribes **Turkish coffee culture and tradition** on the *Representative List of the Intangible Cultural Heritage of Humanity*.

History

Turkish coffee dates back to the Ottoman Empire, where it was first brewed in the 15th century. Coffeehouses, known as *kahvehane*, played a significant role in Ottoman society as places for socialising, intellectual discourse, and entertainment. In the Ottoman Empire, coffeehouses were frequented by writers, scholars, and politicians, contributing to the exchange of ideas and cultural development.

Sultan Murad IV banned coffeehouses in the 17th century, considering them places of political unrest, subversive dissent, and moral corruption.

In Turkish culture, offering coffee to a potential partner is seen as a romantic gesture, often accompanied by the saying '*bir fincan kahvenin kırk yıl hatırı vardır*,' meaning 'a cup of coffee commits one to forty years of friendship.'

While traditional Turkish coffee is served plain or with sugar, there are variations like *menengiç kahvesi* made from roasted pistachios, and *salep*, made from orchid roots.

Turkish coffee became a symbol of cultural diplomacy, with coffeehouses serving as platforms for cultural exchange and understanding worldwide.

Of course, some of us know it as Greek coffee, and some others persist in calling it Byzantine coffee!

16th May 2024

18 Strangelove

Edward Teller: The real Dr Strangelove

'OPPENHEIMER: In a straight race to build the Bomb, the Germans win. We've got one hope.

COLONEL GROVES: Which is?

OPPENHEIMER: Anti-Semitism.'

– *Oppenheimer* (2023), screenplay by Christopher Nolan

Adolf Hitler called Quantum Physics 'the Jewish science'. He didn't trust it. And he could not stomach the thought of these '*Untermensch*' Jews developing something valuable. Hitler was more interested in paganism and magic (and also quack medicine, in his last years). He was a real philistine when it came to science.

The Manhattan Project's race with the Nazis (and the Russians) to build the first nuclear bomb was spurred on by the hope that Hitler, blinded by hate, would deny physicist Werner Heisenberg the proper resources he needed for the German nuclear programme. And so it transpired.

Father of the H-bomb

The Hungarian-born theoretical physicist Edward Teller was a core part of Robert Oppenheimer's team at Los Alamos. After the war, Teller continued his pet project of the much more powerful Hydrogen bomb, and years later he worked on *Excalibur*, the space-based laser which he sold to President Reagan as the ultimate shield against missile attack.

The film director Benny Safdie (*Hidden Gems*) plays Teller in the *Oppenheimer* film - one of the best performances in the movie. The moment when the Bomb is first tested in the desert (the *Trinity test*), the explosion is reflected in Teller's dark glasses, and a diabolical smile spreads across his face. This is director Christopher Nolan's homage to the film *Dr Strangelove*.

Teller became known as the model for Dr Strangelove, the eponymous scientist in Stanley Kubrick's classic black comedy. Teller rejected this association, not least because the Dr Strangelove film character is an unreformed Nazi. Not only was Teller no Nazi, but he also saw the Stalinist influence in Eastern Europe. He was a committed anti-totalitarian.

Born in Budapest in 1908 to Jewish parents, Teller was educated at home and then teased and bullied mercilessly when he eventually went to school. He was gifted, but moving around Europe from one centre of excellence in physics to another, he became an outsider - a brilliant outcast.

Teller believed in 'peace through strength'. He did not want a hydrogen bomb because it would kill more people, but because once it was *possible*, 'it was out of our powers to prevent it'.

By the time the H-bomb had been accepted, Teller believed that Oppenheimer had campaigned against it.

Disarmament

Teller's work can be seen in the 1980s strategic defence initiative ('SDI'), popularly known as the 'Star Wars' programme, and its influential role in the break-up of the Soviet Union.

The Russians took it so seriously that when US President Ronald Reagan first announced it, amazed veteran negotiators at the 1986 Reykjavik summit watched as the Soviet Union's Premier Mikhail Gorbachev offered to eliminate all his nuclear weapons if SDI were confined to the lab for 10 years. That didn't happen, but East-West relations had entered a new phase.

Journalist Matthew d'Ancona has suggested that we should replace the socioeconomic shorthand term *Centrist Dad*, with *Bomb Bloke* – so enamoured is the male of the species with all things nuclear.

Nuclear paranoia was deeply pervasive in the 1940s and 1950s – 'radiation' became a major theme in super-hero comics, and the younger generation rebelled against the perceived betrayal by their elders who 'almost wiped us out.'

There's a direct link from nuclear science and the development of the Bomb to teenage rage, and to beatnik counter-culture, and to the hippy movement ... and to *The Catcher in The Rye* (1951).

5th January 2023

19 Cavafy

Cavafy v. The English: The epic and the miniature

Constantine P. Cavafy (1863–1933) was a Greek poet of the modernist era, celebrated for his profound and innovative writing. Born in Alexandria, Egypt, to a family of Greek descent, Cavafy's work reflects the rich cultural tapestry of Hellenistic history, contemporary issues, and human introspection.

His poems, often intimate and melancholic, explore themes of identity, desire, and the passage of time, setting personal experiences against a backdrop of historical events.

Cavafy's distinct style, characterised by plain diction and ironic undertones, has made him a cornerstone of modern Greek literature. His most famous works, including *Ithaka* - about life's journey, using Odysseus's adventures as the template - and *Waiting for the Barbarians*, resonate universally. Cavafy's ability to bridge ancient and modern sensibilities solidified his importance as a global literary figure.

Cavafy's writing has elements that can be likened to two titans of English poetic literature, Philip Larkin and W.H. Auden.

Larkin first.

Mortality and time

Like Larkin, Cavafy often meditates on the passage of time, the inevitability of aging, and the loss of youth. Poems such as *'The City'* and *'Ithaka'* echo Larkin's obsession with human limitations and the inexorable decline of life, as seen in *'Aubade'* or *'Dockery and Son.'* Both poets confront existential truths with stark clarity.

The ordinary

Cavafy, much like Larkin, finds profundity in the mundane and everyday moments, though his focus is often on historical or personal anecdotes. This approach is similar to Larkin's exploration of the banal realities of life, such as in *'The Whitsun Weddings'*.

Tone of resignation

Both poets convey a melancholic, at times disillusioned, tone. Cavafy's resigned voice in *'The God Abandons Antony'* mirrors Larkin's wry acceptance of life's limits and disappointments.

Minimalism

Both poets favour directness and clarity in language. Cavafy's restrained diction and conversational tone align well with Larkin's avoidance of ornamentation or elaborate stylistic flourishes.

Now W.H. Auden.

Historical and political consciousness

Cavafy's poems, such as *'Waiting for the Barbarians'* and *'The Trojans,'* reflect an acute awareness of history and collective experience, much like Auden's works *'Spain 1937'* and *'The Shield of Achilles'*. Both poets interweave individual experience with larger cultural or historical narratives.

Exploring identity

Cavafy's treatment of identity – particularly sexual identity – resonates with Auden's engagement with themes of love, self-awareness, and the complexities of desire. In poems like *'In the Tavernas'* and *'Days of 1903,'* Cavafy's exploration of longing and memory mirrors Auden's candid discussions of love in works like *'Lullaby'*.

Use of myth and archetype

Cavafy often invokes mythological and historical figures to explore timeless human struggles, as in *'Thermopylae'* or *'Waiting for the Barbarians.'* This recalls Auden's use of classical references and allegory to give his poems a broader philosophical resonance, as seen in *'Musée des Beaux Arts'*.

Experiments

Though not as structurally diverse as Auden, Cavafy shares a tendency to experiment within a formal framework. His incorporation of free verse and unconventional stanza arrangements parallels Auden's adaptability and willingness to vary his style.

Closer to Auden?

While Cavafy shares Larkin's introspection and focus on time, his broader engagement with history, identity, and myth aligns him more closely with W.H. Auden.

Both Cavafy and Auden address universal themes through specific cultural lenses, often balancing personal reflection with broader philosophical or historical concerns.

Cavafy's fascination with history and his ability to universalise the personal and political situate him firmly in the tradition of Auden's expansive poetic vision.

Cavafy and Larkin are poets of failure, disappointment, nostalgia and the outsider looking in.

Auden is at the centre, defining the zeitgeist for everyone. Not something that can be said of Cavafy.

Test

If you had shown me the following few lines blind, and asked me to name the author, I'd have guessed wrongly that it was Cavafy: -

'In Brueghel's *Icarus*, for instance: how everything turns away

Quite leisurely from the disaster; the ploughman may
Have heard the splash, the forsaken cry,
But for him it was not an important failure;
The expensive delicate ship that must have seen
Something amazing, a boy falling out of the sky,
Had somewhere to get to and sailed calmly on.'

– from Auden's *Musée des Beaux Arts,* December 1938

23rd December 2024

V – Music

'A gentleman is someone who can play the accordion, but doesn't.'

— Tom Waits

20 Soul

'A Change is Gonna Come'

- Sam Cooke

The Northern Soul movement started in the late 1960s / early 1970s, in the north of England.

It was a working class scene of the northern industrial towns - Manchester, Blackburn, Wigan, Stoke, Bolton, and Blackpool.

It was basically started by young men who travelled down to London for football matches. Whilst in London, they would visit a shop called *Soul City* in Covent Garden. They were looking for obscure soul records. They loved the pace, energy and romantic lyricism of Motown. The sound and speed of the *Four Tops* being especially popular. But they wanted less commercial tracks, less mainstream songs.

The shop was run by the soul music collector Dave Godin. Godin coined the phrase in his weekly column in *Blues & Soul* in June 1970. He says, 'I started to notice that northern football fans who were in London to follow their team were coming into the store to buy records, but they weren't interested in the latest hits. I devised the name as a shorthand sales term. You've got customers from the north, don't waste time playing them records in the US charts, just play them what they like - Northern Soul'.

The stories and lyrics of the 'back streets' of Detroit depicted in the songs found strong resonance and affinity with the working class experience of northern England.

They played the records in their dance clubs back home - venues such as the *Twisted Wheel* in Manchester, the *Wigan Casino* and *Blackpool Mecca* - and this developed into a distinctive, high-octane, high-energy dance craze. Some of these moves made their way into break-dancing and Hip-hop.

Some of the key songs of Northern Soul scene were *Tainted Love* by Gloria Jones, *Wade in the Water* by Marlena Shaw and *Heatwave* by *Martha Reeves & the Vandellas.* The talismanic template, however, was *I Can't Help Myself* by the *Four Tops,* which was a four beat, ultra-fast stomper, with the aching vocals of legendary lead singer Levi Stubbs, and a snare on every drumbeat.

Fashion

A large proportion of Northern Soul's original audience came from the 1960s mod subculture. Two sub-strands emerged: skinheads and the northern soul scene.

Early Northern Soul fashion included strong elements of the classic mod style, such as button-down Fred Perry and Ben Sherman shirts and polo-shirts, brogue shoes and shrink-to-fit Levi's jeans. Later, Northern Soul dancers started to wear light and loose-fitting clothing for reasons of practicality.

The clenched raised fist symbol that became associated with the Northern Soul movement emanates from the 1960s Black Power movement in the United States. Many dancers wore black gloves, and in between records one would hear the occasional cry of 'right on now!'

Cultural legacy

Another development that we can trace from that era to the modern day, is the central figure of the DJ. Some key DJ's at the time within this scene were Pete Waterman and Peter Stringfellow, who went on to respectively become kings of pop and London nightclubs.

Like the superstar DJ's of today, the Northern Soul DJs built up a following based on satisfying the crowd's desire for music they could not hear anywhere else. The competitiveness between DJs to unearth 'in-demand' sounds led them to cover up the labels on their records, giving rise to the modern white label pressing.

Many argue that northern soul was instrumental in creating a network of clubs, record collectors and dealers in the UK. It was the first music scene to provide the British charts with records that sold entirely on the strength of club play.

2nd November 2023

21 Kraftwerk

Electric dreams: How Kraftwerk wired the world for sound

In the realm of electronic music, few names resonate with as much legendary weight as Kraftwerk.

Emerging from Düsseldorf, Germany, in the early 1970s, Kraftwerk didn't just play music; they crafted a new soundscape, a futuristic vision where man and machine coalesced. The group, founded by Ralf Hütter and Florian Schneider, adopted a reclusive, enigmatic presence, shunning the typical rock star limelight in favour of an image as faceless architects of the future. They founded Kling Klang Studios, through which they recorded and released their music.

Kraftwerk's influence can be heard echoing through decades of music. They were pioneers of the synthesizer revolution, introducing a blend of minimalist electronic beats, robotic vocals, and sequencers. Their groundbreaking albums like 'Autobahn' (1974), 'Trans-Europe Express' (1977), 'The Man-Machine' (1978) and 'Computer World' (1981) weren't just records; they were soundtracks to a world where technology harmonised with human experience.

The group's penchant for seclusion added to their mystique. Rarely giving interviews and preferring to let their meticulously crafted sounds and visuals speak for them, Kraftwerk became mythical figures in the music world. This reticence did not diminish their influence; it magnified it. Their music, embodying themes of urbanisation, travel, and the digital age, resonated with generations looking toward the future.

Kraftwerk's sonic innovations laid the groundwork for an array of genres and artists. The group's mechanical rhythms and synthesized melodies can be seen as the DNA of genres like techno, electro, and synth-pop. Detroit producers like Juan Atkins, Derrick May, and Kevin Saunderson cited Kraftwerk as a primary influence. Atkins referred to them as the 'Beatles of electronic dance music.'

I remember buzzing with excitement when I first heard their number one hit *The Model*. The uniqueness of it.

The influence didn't stop at genre creation; it pervaded mainstream and underground music alike. David Bowie was inspired by Kraftwerk in his 'Berlin Trilogy.' The track 'V-2 Schneider' from Bowie's album 'Heroes' is a direct homage to Kraftwerk's Florian Schneider.

Hip-hop artists like Afrika Bambaataa sampled Kraftwerk's work, with their iconic 'Planet Rock' borrowing from 'Trans-Europe Express.' This cross-pollination of electronic and hip-hop elements helped shape the burgeoning hip-hop scene. Jay-Z used a sample from Man-Machine on his '(Always Be My) Sunshine' in 1997.

Other artists influenced by Kraftwerk include Daft Punk, Fergie, Beck, Neil Young, La Roux, and Coldplay, who sampled 'Computer Love' for their song 'Talk.' New Order used a monk chant from Kraftwerk's track 'Uranium' on their 1983 mega-hit 'Blue Monday'.

The band have seen some lineup changes over the years, and continue to perform live around the world, with their 3D concerts offering a sensory experience that melds music, visuals, and technology. Despite the passing of co-founder Florian Schneider in 2020, Kraftwerk's remaining members, led by Ralf Hütter, persist in exploring the intersection of humanity and technology.

The 3D concert series at New York's Museum of Modern Art (MoMA) in 2012 was followed by further presentations at Tate Modern Turbine Hall (London), Akasaka Blitz (Tokyo), Opera House (Sydney), Foundation Louis Vuitton (Paris), and Guggenheim Museum (Bilbao). In 2014 Ralf Hütter was honoured with the Grammy Lifetime Achievement Award.

Their influence extends beyond music into the realms of culture and technology. Kraftwerk's work anticipated the digital revolution and the advent of the internet age, embedding themselves into the cultural consciousness as prophets of a new era. The band's aesthetic, characterised by its clean, minimalist design and futuristic themes, continues to inspire visual artists and designers.

Kraftwerk's legacy endures as a testament to their pioneering spirit and unparalleled impact on the musical landscape.

2nd November 2023

22 War

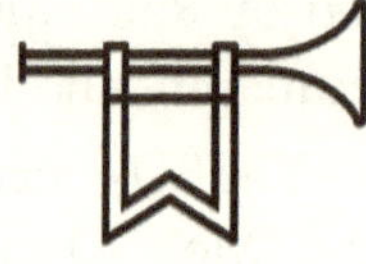

Battle music

Her late Majesty Queen Elizabeth II once approached and cornered the Chancellor of the Exchequer, George Osborne, at a state dinner.

She said to him: *'The Chief of Defence Staff is unable to answer my question. He told me to go and speak to the Defence Secretary. I went to see the Defence Secretary, and he told me to come and speak to you. So I'm asking you. You're not going to close, are you, the Highland Bagpipe school of the British Army?'*

George Osborne gasped, *'Of course not, Your Majesty.'*

The next day Osborne gets into work at the Treasury, and asked his private office, *'Is there a bagpipe school? And for God's sake, tell me we're not closing it down.'*

Nobody knew immediately. So off they scurried, deep into the Treasury, to find out.

They reported back that, yes, apparently there is a Highland Music school as part of the Army bands, and that there *were* some cuts being planned.

Osborne replied, *'Well, we're not making those cuts anymore.'*

Osborne immediately sent a message back to the Palace, informing Her Majesty that she could be reassured that the pipers of British Army would remain well trained.

Signals

Music has long been intertwined with war and armies, serving practical, ceremonial, and psychological functions. From ancient times to the modern day, it has played an essential role in communication, morale-boosting, and cultural identity.

Before modern communication technologies, armies used music as a practical tool. Instruments such as drums, bugles, and trumpets conveyed orders over long distances during battles, signalling commands like attack, retreat, or assembly. Examples include Roman war horns (*cornu*), Napoleonic military drums, and the bugle calls used by modern armies.

Music has always been used to inspire troops, maintain morale, and instil unity. Soldiers marching to music developed a sense of rhythm and cohesion, which could reduce fatigue and encourage teamwork. Songs like '*Over There*' in World War I or '*The Ballad of the Green Berets*' in the Vietnam War boosted optimism and determination at home and on the frontlines.

Certain instruments, such as Scottish bagpipes or war drums, were used for their psychological impact on enemies, to intimidate them. Their loud, distinctive sounds created an atmosphere of fear and chaos before battles.

Military music is also a cornerstone of remembrance. Bugle calls like '*The Last Post*' are used in funerals and commemorations, while marches celebrate victories and honour fallen soldiers.

Highland music

The bagpipe is deeply rooted in Scottish culture and became a hallmark of Highland regiments in the British Army from the 18th century onward. Bagpipes were used to inspire troops and intimidate enemies.

During battles, pipers would play as soldiers advanced, their music providing a sense of bravery and unity. For example, during the Battle of Waterloo (1815), pipers famously played under fire.

During the D-Day Landings (1944), Bill Millin, a personal piper to Lord Lovat, played the bagpipes during the Normandy invasion, defying German fire. His playing inspired Allied troops and added to his legend, as German snipers reportedly refrained from targeting him, believing him to be 'mad.'

The Highland music school within the British Army was established to formalise the training of pipers and drummers, ensuring the preservation of Scottish musical traditions while integrating them into military life. The school helped maintain the high standard of performance required for military parades, ceremonies, and combat operations.

Pipers and drummers in the British Army learn traditional Scottish music, such as marches, reels, and laments, alongside techniques specific to military performances. They are trained to perform in military bands, regimental gatherings, and ceremonial events, both domestically and internationally.

Modern times

Today, the role of Highland music in the British Army has shifted from battlefield use to ceremonial and cultural functions. Bagpipers and drummers are now iconic symbols of regimental identity, performing in parades, state occasions, and military tattoos (e.g., the Royal Edinburgh Military Tattoo).

Highland music remains an integral part of regimental traditions, fostering pride and connection among soldiers while promoting Scottish heritage worldwide.

Music has always been central to the experience of war, both practically and emotionally. Highland music, particularly the bagpipe tradition, is a unique and iconic aspect of this relationship, blending cultural inheritance with military discipline.

The Highland music school within British Army bands ensures this legacy endures, adapting a centuries-old tradition to modern ceremonial and cultural contexts.

6th January 2025

23 Blind

Homer and The Blues

'Sing to me, Muse, of that endlessly cunning man
Who was blown off course to the ends of the earth'
— The Odyssey, translated by Stephen Mitchell

Blues music originated in the Deep South of the United States in the late 19th century, rooted in African American 'spirituals', work songs, and folk traditions. It is characterised by its soulful expression of emotion, often reflecting themes of hardship and resilience, using a distinctive 12-bar structure, 'blue' notes, and lyrical call-and-response patterns.

Blind singers in the Blues and Gospel music traditions in America included Blind Lemon Jefferson, Blind Willie Johnson, Blind Blake, and the Reverend Gary Davis. Blindness often pushed these artists toward careers as musicians, as physical labour was inaccessible. They became storytellers for their communities, expressing the struggles, hopes, and cultural identity of African Americans.

Shared elements

There is a palpable connection between The Blues, blind singers and the long history of oral storytelling, starting from Homer himself. It lies in the shared traditions of verbal dexterity and memory, performance, and the unique cultural roles of blind artists as carriers of communal memory and emotion.

Homer, the ancient Greek poet, composer of *The Iliad* and *The Odyssey,* is often depicted as blind in classical tradition. His epics were part of a tradition where poets (or 'rhapsodes') memorised and performed long narratives, often accompanied by music or rhythm. These tales preserved the history, myths, and cultural values of ancient Greece and were performed for live audiences, similar to musical or poetic performances.

Likewise, Blues musicians captured the experiences of marginalised communities in the American South. Both served as oral historians - cultural memory keepers - transforming lived experiences into art.

Homeric tales and blues songs often explore universal themes of struggle, loss, exile, journeys and resilience. Just as Homer's characters endure suffering, blues songs articulate pain, perseverance and survival, often in deeply personal terms.

Homer used formulaic phrases and improvisation to adapt his epics to audiences. Blues musicians also improvised lyrics and melodies, creating dynamic, responsive performances.

Blindness is often seen as a metaphor for inner vision, suggesting that true insight comes from beyond mere physical sight. Blindness also holds profound significance in the works of John Milton and Jorge Luis Borges, shaping their literary work.

John Milton, the English poet, became blind later in life, and this loss deeply influenced his work, particularly

Paradise Lost. Milton's blindness forced him to '*see*' inwardly, leading to a profound exploration of spiritual and moral themes. In the poem, Milton even speaks through the character of Samson, expressing his personal struggle with blindness as both a physical limitation and a source of spiritual strength.

Jorge Luis Borges, the Argentine writer, also went blind later in life. This loss sharpened his philosophical explorations of infinity, time, and the labyrinthine nature of human existence. Borges saw blindness as a gift that pushed him towards deeper intellectual and imaginative realms, as evidenced in his intricate stories and essays.

Just as Homer contributed to the cultural identity of ancient Greeks by celebrating their heroic past, blues music helped forge a sense of identity and unity within the African American community. The music expressed shared experiences and struggles, fostering solidarity.

Tiresias

The theme of blindness in classical antiquity is repeatedly embodied in the character of Tiresias. Tiresias is a revered figure in Greek mythology, known for his wisdom and his gift of prophecy, which he acquired alongside his blindness.

Tiresias' blindness is explained in several myths. One version recounts that he was blinded by Hera for revealing that women experience greater pleasure than men during sexual intercourse, a judgment he made after living as both a man and a woman.

In compensation for his blindness, Zeus (or Apollo, in some versions) granted Tiresias the ability to foresee the future, and he was gifted an extended lifespan and the ability to communicate with the dead. Tiresias' blindness symbolises his detachment from the distractions of the physical world, enhancing his spiritual and moral insight.

Tiresias plays significant roles in several works of classical literature, including '*The Odyssey*', where Odysseus ventures to the Underworld to seek his guidance. Tiresias foretells Odysseus' challenges, including the dangers of the journey home and the fate of his crew.

Tiresias also plays a prominent role in Sophocles' Theban plays: in '*Oedipus the King*' he reveals the truth of Oedipus' patricide and incest. In '*Antigone*', Tiresias warns King Creon of the dire consequences of his refusal to bury Polynices and his punishment of Antigone. His prophecy prompts Creon to reconsider his actions, though it is too late to avert tragedy.

Tiresias serves as a voice of truth, often unheeded until calamity strikes, underscoring the perils of ignoring wisdom.

Prophecy

In the Coen Brothers film, '*O Brother, Where Art Thou?*' (2000), there is a blind character who is an unnamed *blind seer*, played by Lee Weaver.

He appears as a railroad handcar operator who gives cryptic, prophetic advice to the main characters – Everett, Pete, and Delmar. The character is inspired by Tiresias (fused with Homer himself), aligning with the film's overall loose adaptation of Homer's *Odyssey*.

The blind seer delivers enigmatic lines that set the tone for the protagonists' journey:

'You seek a great fortune, you three who are now in chains. And you will find a fortune, though it will not be the one you seek.'

This foreshadows the characters' transformative journey. Although they initially seek buried treasure, their true 'fortune' is redemption and reconciliation.

Our journeys contain more than meets the eye.

17th January 2025

VI - Drama

'The play's the thing.'

- Hamlet, II, 2

24 Dawn

'Rosy-fingered dawn': And repeat

New translations of 2,800-year-old Homer appear each year. Emily Wilson's has been one of the most acclaimed recent additions.

The Iliad and *The Odyssey* often have repeated, stock phrases, like: 'sparkly eyed Athena', 'spring-heeled Achilles', 'swift-footed horses', 'resourceful Odysseus', and 'wine-red sea'.

Dawn appears thirty times in *The Odyssey.* A new day arrives, alive with possibilities, and the same line is repeated, word for word, each time: **ήμος δ' ηριγένεια φάνη *ροδοδάκτυλος Ηώς***: which translates to 'when early-born *rosy-fingered Dawn* appeared…'

These repetitions suggest that things have an eternal, infinitely ritualistic presence. Different things will happen every day, but Dawn always appears, always with rosy fingers, always early.

Wilson plays with this repetition by varying the translation according to the context.

In an oral, or semiliterate culture, repeated epithets gave the listener an anchor in a quick-moving story. In a more literate society such as ours, repetitions may feel like moments to skip. They can be writerly laziness, and bore the reader. Wilson explores the multiple connotations of each phrase.

Here are Wilson's differing translations, of all thirty appearances of Dawn in *The Odyssey*:-

- The early Dawn was born; her fingers bloomed
- When newborn Dawn appeared with rosy fingers
- When rosy-fingered Dawn came bright and early
- Soon Dawn was born, her fingers bright with roses
- When Dawn appeared, her fingers bright with flowers
- When early Dawn appeared and touched the sky with blossom
- Then Dawn rose up from bed with Lord Tithonus, to bring the light to deathless gods and mortals
- When vernal Dawn first touched the sky with flowers
- But when the Dawn with dazzling braids brought day for the third time
- Then Dawn came from her lovely throne, and woke the girl
- Soon Dawn appeared and touched the sky with roses
- When bright-haired Dawn brought the third morning
- When early Dawn shone forth with rosy fingers
- But when the rosy hands of Dawn appeared
- Early the Dawn appeared, pink fingers blooming
- When early Dawn revealed her rose-red hands

- Then when rose-fingered Dawn came, bright and early
- On the third morning brought by braided Dawn
- Then the roses of Dawn's fingers appeared again
- Dawn on her golden throne began to shine
- When Dawn came, born early, with her fingertips like petals
- The golden throne of Dawn was riding up the sky
- When rose-fingered Dawn appeared
- Then Dawn was born again; her fingers bloomed
- Then all at once Dawn on her golden throne lit up the sky
- Dawn soon arrived upon her throne
- When new-born Dawn appeared with hands of flowers
- When early Dawn, the new-born child with rosy hands, appeared
- As she said this, the golden Dawn arrived
- She roused the new-born Dawn from Ocean's streams to bring the golden light to those on earth

Homer's association of the word *finger* with its action of *touch,* allows the listener (in Homer's day), and the reader (today), to connect to a sensation, which implies some movement or action or event.

Hence the phrase *'rosy-fingered'* gives us a physical feeling of something natural being experienced through human senses. As finger is to touch, so foot can mean motion or journey.

Shakespeare borrowed this *touch* metaphor from Homer.

Iliad Book 7 line 421: 'The *sun was freshly striking* the fields'.

Hamlet, Act IV, Scene 1: 'The *sun no sooner shall the mountains touch,* but we will ship him hence'.

But, if Homer was blind ...

How could he know that the sun rise was 'rosy fingered', or that the sea was 'wine red'?

The poetic descriptions in Homer's Iliad and Odyssey, such as the 'rosy-fingered dawn' or the 'wine-dark sea,' are among the most famous examples of his vivid and evocative imagery. While it's widely believed that Homer may have been blind, there are a couple of ways to interpret how he could have described such vivid details.

Cultural and descriptive tradition: Even if Homer was blind, it's important to recognise that his works were part of an oral tradition passed down over generations. He might have drawn on centuries of collective knowledge, stories, and shared experiences of people who could see. These descriptions could have been based on the perceptions of others, which he incorporated into his poetry to evoke emotions or convey a sense of beauty and grandeur.

Metaphor and sensory substitution: The 'rosy-fingered dawn' could be seen as a metaphor derived from other sensory experiences. Homer could have heard descriptions of dawn, where the pinkish light may have been associated with soft, delicate fingers. Similarly, the 'wine-dark sea' could be a metaphor for the deep, rich hues of the sea that others experienced, which Homer might have interpreted based on the sensations he could still access – like the sounds and the tactile sensations of the sea, its saltiness, and the waves.

Auditory and tactile perception: Homer might have been particularly sensitive to the other senses, such as sound and touch. He could have heard the descriptions of the world around him and used these to create vivid imagery in his mind. The tactile sense of soft fingers or the feeling of waves could have contributed to his poetic imagery, even if he couldn't physically see these phenomena himself.

Symbolic language: Homer was likely using symbolic language to convey certain qualities of things, rather than directly describing what he could see - symbolism for the gentle and gradual nature of the sun's rise, and the vast and mysterious depth of the ocean.

His genius lies in how he could transform the experiences of the world into something universal; transcending the limitations of his own perception.

9th May 2024

25 Lehman

Epic minimalism

Nineteen Sixth-Formers of the St Thomas More School, Wood Green, London, enjoyed a memorable evening at the theatre on Tuesday, 17th December, 2024, in Covent Garden, with a visit to see the magnificent and exhilarating play, '*The Lehman Trilogy*'.

The play tells the story of three brothers who arrived in America in 1844 and built one of the world's largest banks – starting from a humble fabric shop, and then investing in cotton, coffee, railroads, canals, cinema, construction, computers, television and pretty much building the twentieth century. Their collapse in 2009 marked the end of a dynasty that echoes to this day.

The students were enthused and enthralled by the play and marvelled at the cast of just 3 actors playing all 53 characters over an epic 3 hours and 20 minutes.

Students of Economics, History, Business, Sociology and Politics found the evening an enriching cultural experience.

The Tony-winning play has returned to London for a limited run. Golden Globe, Academy Award, and Tony-winner Sam Mendes (director of *Skyfall, American Beauty, 1917* and *Road to Perdition*) returned to direct the production.

In three parts, the play dives into the historical rise and fall of a business from the 19th to the 21st century.

Giving specific context on the 2008 market crash that reverberated around the world, the play follows the inside story of a pivotal player in this event - Lehman Brothers Holdings.

John Heffernan, Aaron Krohn, and Howard W. Overshown bring virtuoso performances.

Based on the works of playwrights Stefano Massini and Ben Power, the saga on the global financial crisis and a large company in the middle of the storm, is underlined by astute observations on the capitalist world order.

Storyline

It's 2008, and the global economy is facing its worst downturn. The American real estate market is crashing, as investment conglomerates and ordinary people face bankruptcy.

The comic scene where a succession of would-be wives are auditioning for ultra-perfectionist Philip Lehman has Chaplinesque poise.

The performances are note-perfect. As we watch the founders Henry, Emanuel and Maver build up their business in 1840s Alabama, making much of their money from cotton, we see Jewish immigrants adjusting to the manners of the New World before they set off to conquer the commanding heights of Wall Street.

The intrigues and deals are played out in Es Devlin's handsome glass box, which, pitched on a revolving stage, becomes almost a character in its own right. Luke Halls's video designs create a stunning backdrop of ever-changing vistas. The Gillian Lynne Theatre is the ideal setting for a drama set amid the concrete and glass canyons of New York. The pianist provides genteel accompaniment from an upright piano at the front of the stalls.

The Wall Street Crash of 1929 becomes a near-death experience for the firm. In the 1960s, Bobbie Lehman, his eyes hidden behind hipster shades, is the last family survivor, surfing the zeitgeist as he dances the twist. It prefigures the death spiral experienced by the firm in the final segment, where the Lehman juggernaut hurtles towards its doom.

Cast and crew

John Heffernan as Henry Lehman

Aaron Krohn as Mayer Lehman

Howard W. Overshown as Emanuel Lehman

Cat Beveridge as Principal Pianist

Book: Stefano Massini

Adapted by: Ben Power

Director: Sam Mendes

Set Design: Es Devlin

28th December 2024

26 Tarantino

Applying Game Theory to the Mexican standoff

Quentin Tarantino's films are known for their intricate and intense *Mexican standoffs,* where participants point guns or knives at each other - and sometimes, cans of dogfood. These often feature high stakes, multiple participants, and hidden motives.

In economics, 'Game Theory' is the study of decision-making where individuals or groups (known as 'players') make choices that affect each other's outcomes. It analyses how participants anticipate others' actions and adjust their decisions to maximise their payoffs.

The practical uses of Game Theory in economics include: *Market competition,* where firms predict pricing and decide their production strategies; *Auctions,* by designing bidding strategies; *Negotiations,* to guide trade deals or wage discussions; *Public policy,* by allocating resources or designing incentives (e.g. carbon credits); and *Behavioural economics,* to understand how people make decisions under risk or uncertainty.

Game Theory has been made famous by some prominent economists: -

- Richard Thaler, who advised on the film *'The Big Short'*, and plays a cameo part in it, as himself. He won the Nobel prize in 2017;
- John Nash, who is also a Nobel Prize winner. He was played by Russell Crowe in *'A Beautiful Mind'*. Nash developed the principle of *compromise* which became known as the *'Nash Equilibrium'*; and
- Yanis Varoufakis, who specialised in Game Theory in his academic work, and then applied it in his short-lived political career helping Greece out of its financial crisis in 2015.

Game Theory themes in Tarantino's standoffs

Common features that are *economic* in nature, appear in the *Mexican standoff* scenes in Tarantino's films: -

- *'Asymmetric information'*: Participants often lack knowledge; and more specifically, they don't have complete knowledge of others' motives, leading to sub-optimal decisions. This is a common constraint in economics.
- *'Trust and cooperation'*: Most standoffs show a failure to establish trust, resulting in mutual losses.
- *'Dominant strategies'*: Pre-emptive violence often dominates, creating the so-called 'prisoner's dilemma' scenario. If two 'prisoners' both confess, they get medium sentences (5 years); if one betrays the other he walks free (0 years) and the other prisoner get a heavier sentence (20 years); if they both remain silent, they get a moderate sentence (1 year).

- *'Outcomes'*: The standoffs generally end in a *'Nash equilibrium'*, where no participant can unilaterally improve their outcome without making things worse for everyone.

Scenarios

Here is a breakdown of some of Tarantino's most notorious Mexican standoff scenes, through the lens of Game Theory.

1. *Reservoir Dogs (1992): The final warehouse scene*

Participants: Joe, Eddie (Joe's son), Mr. White, and Mr. Orange.

Setup:

- Joe accuses Mr. Orange of being a cop.
- Mr. White defends Mr. Orange and threatens Joe.
- Eddie sides with his father.

Trade-offs:

- Joe: Wants to eliminate the cop to protect himself and his organisation.
- Mr. White: Believes in loyalty and protecting Mr. Orange, despite growing evidence.
- Eddie: Unstinting loyalty to his father, and strong suspicion that Mr. Orange is a cop.
- Mr. Orange: Critically wounded, trying to survive but unable to defend himself directly.

Payoffs:

Each participant risks their life based on their choices (loyalty, trust, or survival).

Dominant strategies:

- Joe: Kill Mr. Orange to remove the threat.

- Mr. White: Protect Mr. Orange, believing his loyalty will pay off.
- Eddie: Support Joe, no matter what.

Outcome:

Everyone shoots. Joe, Eddie, and Mr. White die. Mr. Orange survives temporarily but is ultimately killed (by Mr White, or by the police, I'm not sure which), after confessing to Mr. White.

The lack of trust and mutual suspicions escalate the situation into mutual destruction – a 'classic prisoner's dilemma' where cooperation, and a confession (verifying Mr. Orange's status), could have avoided the bloodbath.

2. *Pulp Fiction (1994): The diner standoff*

Participants: Pumpkin (Tim Roth), Honey Bunny (Amanda Plummer), Jules (Samuel L. Jackson), Vincent (John Travolta).

Setup:

- Pumpkin and Honey Bunny are robbing a diner.
- Jules calmly takes control of the situation after Pumpkin tries to rob him.

Trade-offs:

- Pumpkin and Honey Bunny: Want to escape with money while avoiding harm.
- Jules: Wants to de-escalate and avoid violence, guided by his Damascene conversion to his newfound philosophy.
- Vincent: Ready to escalate violence if needed, but trusts Jules to handle the situation.

Payoffs:

- Pumpkin and Honey Bunny: Maximum payoff is escaping with money. Minimum payoff is getting killed.
- Jules: Maximum payoff is peace and survival. Minimum payoff is escalating violence.

Dominant strategies:

- Jules shifts the equilibrium by taking a non-violent approach, offering a 'Pareto improvement' - colloquially known as at the *80:20 rule*. He proposes they take his wallet and leave.
- Pumpkin and Honey Bunny's best response is to accept the deal, which avoids mutual destruction.

Outcome:

Jules's strategy of de-escalation works, and everyone walks away alive. This showcases the power of breaking away from traditional retaliatory strategies in favour of negotiation.

3. *Inglourious Basterds (2009): Basement tavern standoff*

Participants: Lieutenant Archie Hicox, Stiglitz, Wilhelm (German soldier), Bridget von Hammersmark, and other German soldiers.

Setup:

The Basterds are undercover in a tavern. Hicox inadvertently gives away their cover due to a hand gesture.

Trade-offs:

- Hicox and Basterds: Want to maintain their cover to proceed with their mission.
- German soldiers: Their goal is to identify and eliminate spies.

- Von Hammersmark: Wants to avoid suspicion and ensure the mission's success.

Payoffs:

- The Germans' best payoff is identifying the spies and surviving.
- The Basterds' best payoff is completing their mission without casualties.

Dominant strategies:

- The Basterds and Germans are in a 'tit-for-tat' standoff where each move escalates tensions.
- Cooperation is unstable due to asymmetric information and mistrust.

Outcome:

Everyone dies except Wilhelm and von Hammersmark. This illustrates a 'zero-sum game' where both sides' insistence on eliminating threats leads to mutual destruction.

Tarantino's standoffs consistently emphasise how human emotions, mistrust, and self-interest can often disrupt cooperative solutions, and can lead to catastrophic outcomes. They show how behavioural economics - bias, habits, information gaps, or computational errors - leads individuals to make choices that are not rational, and often do not maximise welfare or utility.

21st January 2025

VII – Technology

'Never trust a computer you can't throw out a window.'

– Steve Wozniak

27 Spies

Eastern whispering

'When two people know a secret, it's no longer a secret.'
— Chinese proverb

On paper, it looked like a fantastic deal. In 2017, the Chinese government offered to spend $100m to build an ornate Chinese garden at the National Arboretum in Washington DC. Complete with temples, pavilions and a 70-foot white pagoda, officials hoped it would attract thousands of tourists.

But then US counterintelligence officials found numerous *red flags*. The pagoda would have been strategically placed on one of the highest points in Washington DC - a perfect spot for intelligence collection.

Alarmingly, China wanted to build the pagoda with materials shipped inside diplomatic pouches, which US Customs cannot examine. Federal officials killed the project before construction was underway.

Since 2017, federal officials have investigated Chinese land purchases near critical infrastructure, in what they saw as clear efforts to plant listening devices near sensitive military and government facilities.

The FBI uncovered Chinese-made Huawei equipment in cell towers near US military bases in the Midwest. The FBI determined that the equipment was capable of capturing and disrupting restricted Defence Department communications, including those used by US Strategic Command, which oversees the country's nuclear weapons.

Huawei equipment has the ability to intercept commercial cell traffic but also the highly restricted airwaves used by the military and disrupt critical US Strategic Command communications, giving the Chinese government a window into America's nuclear arsenal. The external communication from the Huawei equipment that occurs when software is updated could be exploited by the Chinese government.

'This gets into some of the most sensitive things we do,' said one FBI official. 'It would impact our ability for essentially command and control with the nuclear triad.'

Turning doves into hawks

The *Federal Communications Commission* (FCC) banned Huawei and other brands of Chinese made equipment. 'The existence of the investigation at the highest levels turned some doves into hawks,' said one US official.

In 2020, Congress approved $1.9 billion to remove Chinese-made Huawei and ZTE cellular technology across rural America. But two years later, none of that equipment has been removed and local telecoms companies are still waiting for federal reimbursement money.

The FCC received applications to remove 24,000 pieces of Chinese-made communications equipment—but it is $3 billion short of the money it needs to reimburse all eligible companies.

FBI Director Christopher Wray said the FBI opens a new China counterintelligence investigation every 12 hours. 'That's about 2,000 investigations,' said Wray. 'And that's not cyber theft, where they have a bigger hacking programme than that of every other major nation combined, and have stolen more of Americans' personal and corporate data than every nation combined.'

Critics see xenophobic overreach

'Do we treat China as a neutral actor? Then there's some crackpot theory behind every tree,' said Anna Puglisi, senior fellow at Georgetown University's Centre for Security and Emerging Technology. 'However, China has shown us through its policies and actions it is not a neutral actor.'

FBI agents monitor a disturbing pattern along *Interstate 25* in Colorado, Montana, and Nebraska. The heavily trafficked corridor connects the most secretive military installations in the US, including nuclear missile silos.

As Huawei equipment began to proliferate near US military bases, federal investigators started taking notice.

'This government has to do a better job of letting everyone know this is a Communist Party issue, it's not a Chinese people issue,' says Bill Evanina, of the National Counterintelligence and Security Centre. 'And I'll be the first to say that the government has to do better with respect to understanding the Communist Party's intentions are not the same intentions of the Chinese people.'

24th August 2023

28 Tesla

Tesla v. The wife

An abused wife took on *Tesla* over tracking technology. She lost.

San Francisco police Sergeant David Radford contacted *Tesla* in May 2020 with a request on a case: Could the automaker provide data on an alleged stalker's remote access to a vehicle?

A woman had come into the station visibly shaken, according to a police report. She told police that her abusive husband, in violation of a restraining order, was stalking and harassing her using the technology in their 2016 *Tesla Model X*.

The car allows owners to remotely access its location and control other features through a smartphone app. She told police she had discovered a metal baseball bat in the back seat – the same bat the husband had previously used to threaten her, the police report stated.

After Sergeant Radford's request, a *Tesla* service manager replied that remote-access logs were only available within seven days of the events recorded. The investigation stalled.

Cases of technology-enabled stalking involving cars are emerging as automakers add ever-more-sophisticated features, such as location tracking and remote control of functions such as locking doors or honking the horn.

The *Alliance for Automotive Innovation* (AAI), a technology trade group for car makers and suppliers, cited spousal violence as a reason why California regulators should not require carmakers to release location or other personal data under a new state privacy law. The law gives consumers the right to access their personal data being tracked by companies. The trade group argued some car owners might improperly request personal data on other drivers of the same vehicle.

Even before the police were involved, the woman made requests to *Tesla* seeking remote data logs and asking *Tesla* to disable her husband's account. *Tesla* said it could not remove her husband's access to the car's technology because his name remained as co-owner on the vehicle's title.

Tesla prevailed in the lawsuit. The automaker argued she had no proof that her husband used the car's features to stalk her.

The woman and her husband settled the lawsuit in 2023. Their divorce case is pending. The restraining order against the husband remains in effect.

In a separate case, Renée Izambard said in an interview that her then-husband was tracking her on his *Tesla* app after he made comments to her indicating he knew where she had been. Izambard filed for divorce from her husband in 2018 and alleged years of physical and psychological abuse.

Unlike the San Francisco woman, Izambard had her own access to change the account settings and turn off its connection to the internet, so she didn't have to interact with *Tesla*.

Apple launched its *AirTag* location-tracking device in 2021 as a way to help people find lost purses or keys. The small tags can easily be concealed in a car's interior, and soon became a favourite tool for one partner to track another.

Earlier this year, *Apple* and *Google* jointly proposed standardised technology that would alert people who are being tracked without their knowledge through tags or smartphone features. The idea won praise from anti-domestic abuse advocates.

San Francisco Superior Court Judge Curtis Karnow agreed with *Tesla*, writing in a 2022 opinion that both the woman and her husband 'had a right' to use the car technology.

'A jilted partner might fabricate misuse charges to punish the other,' Karnow wrote, adding that the consequences of imposing liability for car manufacturers 'would be broad and incalculable.'

In late 2020, the San Francisco woman was allowed by a family court judge to sell the jointly owned *Tesla*.

4th April 2024

29 Games

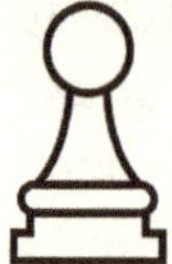

Deep Blue versus Kasparov

'I'm a human being, you know . . . When I see something that is well beyond my understanding, I'm scared.'

– Gary Kasparov

Gary Kasparov is a force of nature. Born in 1963, he was a Russian chess grandmaster and world champion. From 1984 until his retirement from competitive chess in 2005, Kasparov was ranked world number 1 for a record 21 years and 3 months.

He was supremely gifted as a child, but as an adult whenever he walked into a room he was like a tornado, everyone would pin their backs against the wall. They were in awe of this man – sparks just bubbling out of his head.

He was also aware of his own power, and knew how intimidating he was. When he was playing chess against another player he would sit down, take his watch off, and place it on the table. And then he would play. And when he was done toying with you, he'd pick up his watch and return it to his wrist.

Even if you hadn't worked out that you'd lost, he would know that he'd beaten you. That was essentially a message to the room, 'Right, it's done.' And you can either carry on humiliating yourself from that point on, or you can submit.

In 1997, a computer from *IBM* named *Deep Blue* was the first machine to beat this chess grandmaster. The program was very good at this point, but most people agree that Kasparov was still the better chess player. What the computer didn't have was any fear, and it wasn't intimidated by Kasparov. And he wasn't used to this. Suddenly, all of his tricks were useless.

Kasparov hadn't played against a computer before, and hadn't worked out the psychology of how to do this.

So, the IBM researchers did something very clever.

The way the program worked was that it would search through all the different possibilities, so that if it was forced into a particularly tricky position, there would be many more calculations to do. This would take a lot longer for it to churn through them.

The researchers knew that Kasparov knew that if it was tricky, it would take a lot longer to come up with an answer and its next move. So what they did was to deliberately put some code into the program that would *add on a random amount of time* before it came up with an answer. So Kasparov then couldn't tell whether *Deep Blue* was thinking hard, or not thinking at all.

Essentially, the IBM researchers psyched him out. There were points when the machine was waiting for ages and ages, and Kasparov didn't know about this extra little bit of time filler. In situations which seemed like a simple position and the next move was obvious, Kasparov would then wonder, 'What has the machine spotted that I haven't spotted?' And so he started doubting himself and questioning himself. And he says, and others agreed, that that was what led to him making mistakes during the game and eventually losing the match.

The version of *Deep Blue* that defeated Kasparov in 1997 typically searched to a depth of six to eight moves, and twenty or more moves in some situations.

It's not just about the power and the might of computer algorithms versus humans. We have had tools that are super human for ages. Fork lifts are super human. But what happens with Artificial Intelligence is that they make us question ourselves.

3rd August 2023

30 Chaos

You can't unscramble eggs

The Second Law of Thermodynamics states that, sooner or later, everything turns to rat shit. More technically, in a closed system, entropy (or chaos), increases over time.

Put simply, it suggests that systems naturally tend to move from order to disorder, from a state of organisation to a state of randomness or chaos. Just look at the pile of clothes on your exercise bike, or the current state of your desk, or the cleanliness of your car.

As energy is transferred, more and more of it is wasted. It's one of the four laws of thermodynamics, which describe the relationships between heat (thermal energy) and matter.

In summary. 1st Law: energy cannot be created or destroyed; the total *quantity* of energy in the universe stays the same. 2nd Law: any isolated system degenerates into a disordered state. 3rd Law: absolute zero is unreachable. 4th Law: entropy approaches a constant value as temperature approaches zero.

A cup of hot coffee gradually cooling down in a room represents the second law. As its heat disperses, entropy increases in the surroundings.

Crystals are formed from salt as its water evaporates. Crystals are more orderly than salt; however, vapourised water is more disorderly than liquid water. The process results in increased disorder.

Real life

The law also applies to our everyday experience, not just in scientific environments.

Personal human relationships: Without intentional effort invested in maintaining and nurturing relationships, they can deteriorate over time. Just like in thermodynamics, where energy disperses and systems become more disordered, without proactive endeavour, personal relationships can become strained, communication can break down, and conflicts can arise.

Test: How many people from your school days are you still in contact with?

Jobs and careers: In career paths, without continuous learning, growth, and adaptation, one's career can stagnate or decline. Industries evolve, technologies change, job roles shift over time, people move around, and leadership changes often affect performance. Individuals who do not actively adapt and learn new skills may find themselves becoming less effective in their careers.

Sporting prowess: Without regular practice and upkeep, skills can diminish, fitness levels can decline, and performance can suffer. Without ongoing determination, an athlete's abilities may degrade. Ageing will firstly cause an improvement in performance, through increased strength, breathing capacity, stamina and experience. And then, inevitably, ageing will cause a decline in performance, due to fatigue, reduced energy, and longer recovery, as the body's self-maintenance mechanisms become more strained.

Business: Since 1955 there have been over 2,200 companies on the *Fortune 500* list of top corporations. Only 52 of them are still on the list today, that were there on that first list. Companies like *Pfizer, PepsiCo, Exxon, IBM,* and *Boeing,* for example, show that longevity is the exception, not the norm.

Community groups: Whether they're social clubs, volunteer organisations, local committees, sports teams, churches, or choirs, they all tend to disintegrate without active participation, engagement, and organisation. These groups lose momentum and membership dwindles.

It'll all be fine in the end

Eventually, all the energy in the universe will be evenly distributed, leading to a state of maximum entropy, where no energy exists. This is known as the *heat death* of the universe.

Like that cup of hot coffee left out in a room. The heat from the coffee spreads throughout the room until everything reaches the same temperature, and the coffee becomes cold. There will then be no energy available to fuel any processes, life or motion.

Everything will wind down in a few billion years, leaving the universe in a state of complete uniformity and stillness.

Happy days.

6th June 2024

31 Airlines

Clouded costs, ticket trickery: The mysteries of airline pricing

It happens every time you book a flight. You complain about the price. You leave it for a few days, or even a few minutes. Then when you check again, the price has gone up.

Dynamic pricing of airline seats is a common practice in the aviation industry. This involves adjusting ticket prices based on the several influencing factors, such as the level of demand, time until departure, competitiveness of the route, and availability of seats.

This strategy allows airlines to maximise revenue by optimising the pricing of each seat to reflect its perceived value to different passengers. It's a subtle form of discriminatory pricing, and it's legal.

According to economic norms, when demand exceeds supply, prices tend to rise, and conversely, when supply exceeds demand, prices tend to fall. Airlines use this principle by adjusting ticket prices in real-time based on fluctuations in demand and supply. For instance, as the departure date approaches and the number of available seats decreases, airlines may increase prices to capitalise on the scarcity of seats and the heightened need from last-minute travellers.

Conversely, if a flight is not filling up as expected, airlines may lower prices to stimulate interest and fill the remaining seats. The level of demand for a particular flight is influenced by various factors, including the time of booking, seasonality, destination popularity, and the prevailing economic conditions at the time.

During peak travel seasons, with higher demand, ticket prices edge upwards. Similarly, flights to popular destinations or business hubs often experience greater demand, resulting in higher prices. Other factors such as consumer confidence and fuel prices also impact prices.

Flights leaving at 6am tend to be cheaper than more popular times. This also rewards business or frequent travellers for their regular custom and their volume buying of flight travel.

On the supply side, airlines manage their availability of seats across their fleet to optimise revenue while minimising costs. Factors such as aircraft capacity, route network, scheduling constraints, and operational efficiency determine the supply of seats on any given flight.

Airlines strike a balance between maximising the percentage of seats filled on a flight and avoiding overcapacity, which can lead to lower profitability.

Advancements in technology have revolutionised the practice of dynamic pricing. With the advent of sophisticated revenue management systems and algorithms, airlines can analyse vast amounts of data in real-time to forecast demand patterns, segment customers, and adjust pricing dynamically. These systems take into account historical booking data, competitor pricing, customer preferences, and weather conditions, to optimise prices and maximise revenue.

Over time, prices have responded to technological advancements. For example, the proliferation of online booking platforms and mobile applications has led to greater price transparency and competition, forcing airlines to adapt their pricing strategies to remain competitive.

Additionally, liberalisation of the airline industry has led to increased competition and pricing flexibility, allowing airlines to use responsive pricing models.

Deliberate overbooking is a common practice. It is normal for a small percentage of passengers to just *not show up* – for domestic flights this can be up to 10% (it's slightly lower for international flights). When all passengers turn up, and the flight is already full, airlines may offer an alternative flight, with a hotel stay or a free lunch voucher.

And then there are hidden charges. The top culprits are: extra prices for luggage, booking fees, credit card fees, quoting prices without tax, printing of boarding cards, in-flight snacks, seat reservations, extra legroom, online check-in and priority boarding.

18th July 2024

32 VW

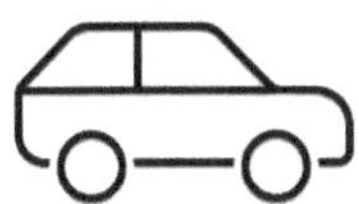

Saving Private Volkswagen

'I gave back my Tesla and bought an electric VW instead.'
— Alyssa Milano, actress, November 2024

If you thought the founder of Tesla was bad, wait till you find out who founded Volkswagen. How's this for virtue signalling?

Volkswagen (VW) was founded in 1937 by the German Labour Front (Deutsche Arbeitsfront), a Nazi-affiliated organisation, under the leadership of Adolf Hitler.

The company was initially established as a key component of Nazi propaganda, aiming to produce an affordable *'people's car'* (*Volks wagen*) for the German population.

Ferdinand Porsche, an engineer, played a crucial role in designing the original VW Beetle. The project was promoted and funded by the Nazi regime.

Volkswagen was created as part of Hitler's vision for a motorised Germany. During World War II, Volkswagen shifted from producing civilian vehicles to manufacturing military transportation equipment and vehicles.

The company relied heavily on forced labour, including prisoners of war, concentration camp inmates, and foreign civilians. Tens of thousands of forced labourers were exploited in VW factories under inhumane conditions.

Circumstance, not ideology

Some historians argue that Volkswagen, like many other German companies (e.g., BMW and Siemens), operated under the extreme pressures of a totalitarian state and had little choice but to comply with Nazi policies.

Ferdinand Porsche and other engineers associated with the company may not have been ideologically aligned with the Nazis but were pragmatically working within the framework imposed by the regime. Much like the technocrats in Saddam Hussein's Iraq, under the *Ba'athist* regime - librarians, lecturers, engineers - who were just doing their job.

Before the war, Volkswagen's concept of a 'people's car' was seen as a progressive industrial idea for its time — mass-producing affordable vehicles for ordinary people. The vision itself wasn't inherently tied to Nazi ideology, even if it was co-opted by Hitler as propaganda.

British control

Volkswagen's factory had been heavily bombed, and after World War II, the company was effectively leaderless and financially devastated.

The town of Wolfsburg, where the factory was located, fell under British occupation in 1945. The factory was initially set to be dismantled as part of the Allies' policy of *'de-Nazification'*, effectively deindustrialising Germany to prevent future militarisation.

Major Ivan Hirst, a British Army officer, played a critical role in sparing the plant. He recognised the factory's potential to produce civilian vehicles and proposed using it to fulfil transportation needs for the British and Allied forces.

In 1945, Hirst oversaw the repair and reorganisation of the factory. Despite post-war shortages of materials and workers, Volkswagen began producing the Type 1, known as the Beetle.

By 1946, Volkswagen began producing cars for the civilian market, though the company still operated under British military oversight.

The Beetle, originally designed in the 1930s under Ferdinand Porsche, became the cornerstone of this revival. Its simple, reliable design and affordability made it an attractive option for post-war consumers.

Volkswagen's growth

The factory was returned to German control in 1949. The newly established Federal Republic of Germany (West Germany) took ownership, and the company became a state-controlled enterprise.

In the 1950s, the Beetle became a symbol of Germany's recovery (the 'Wirtschaftswunder' or economic miracle). It was exported to multiple countries, including the United States, where it became an iconic vehicle.

In the 1960s, Volkswagen transitioned from a state-controlled enterprise to a publicly traded company, eventually becoming one of the world's largest automakers. At one point in 2008, VW became the most valuable company in the world, when a surge in its share price hit €1,000, and its market valuation reached €300bn.

The period of British control is widely credited with saving Volkswagen.

2nd December 2024

33 Bats

Bat shed crazy: The colossal cost of high-speed waste

'People say you've gone over the budget, but did people think about the bats?'

— Sir Jon Thompson, Chairman, HS2

The economy of the United Kingdon has been growing at a modest 1.5% per annum for the last 20 years. China clocks in at 9%, India at 5% and the USA at 3%.

Rather than embracing entrepreneurialism, innovation and free trade, there seems to be a culture of regulation, consultation, and middle management lethargy in the UK.

High speed rail

One public infrastructure project which should have boosted Britain's prospects and growth is the HS2 (High Speed 2) rail link, intended to connect London, Birmingham, Manchester, and Leeds.

But it has seen substantial budget increases and delays since its inception.

The HS2 project was originally estimated to cost around £33 billion when it was first approved in 2012. Over the years, costs escalated significantly. By 2019, the estimated cost had risen to £106 billion due to rising land, labour, and materials costs, as well as the burden of regulation and complying with ever more bizarre laws. By 2023 the estimate had reached £120 billion.

An estimated £24 billion has already been spent on the programme. This includes expenses for land purchases, construction of initial phases, planning, and preparatory works.

Bats

One of the most absurd lines of expenditure has been the £100 million spent on bat conservation measures, including a 'bat barn'.

One might see this as HS2's commitment to meeting strict environmental and wildlife regulations. The UK has stringent laws regarding the protection of endangered species, including bats.

As a result, HS2 was required to build habitats, tunnels, and even barns to ensure the preservation of wildlife disrupted by construction. The bat barn and other similar expenses became a controversial symbol of excessive costs due to regulatory and compliance demands. Supporters view it as necessary environmental stewardship.

The curved bat shed structure runs for around one kilometre alongside Sheephouse Wood, in Buckinghamshire, creating a barrier allowing the local colony of Bechstein's bats to cross above the high-speed railway without being affected by passing trains.

Other more expensive options, including a bored tunnel and re-routing the railway away from the wood, were considered during the passage of the *High Speed Two (London to West Midlands) Act* through Parliament.

HS2 spent 'hundreds of thousands of pounds' on lawyers and environmental specialists. This is an example of the UK's genuine problem with completing major infrastructure projects.

HS2 has been required to obtain 8,276 consents from other public bodies related to planning, transport and the environment to build phase one of the railway between the capital and Birmingham.

HS2 told a rail industry conference the bat protection structure is needed to appease the Government adviser *Natural England,* despite there being 'no evidence that high-speed trains interfere with bats'.

As if this story isn't absurd enough already, it turns out that the number of bats affected was vastly over-estimated. So, in the end, the shed cost around £300,000 per bat.

Opportunity cost

How many new homes could have been built with this £100 million?

The typical cost of building a home in the UK varies significantly based on location and size. Using a mid-range estimate of £200,000 per home, the £100 million spent on the bat shed could have potentially funded the construction of around 500 new homes.

The 'bat shed' exemplifies the complex challenges and regulatory hurdles faced during the HS2 project's development.

In December 2024 the structure was completed, amid ongoing debates over cost and necessity.

The *EDF Energy* nuclear power plant at Hinkley Point in Somerset has similar challenges. In their case, it isn't bats. It's badgers.

The UK has become a figure of fun around the world. We no longer have any authority or a serious presence on the world stage. We are a Monty Python parody. A former world power reduced to pushing Orwellian laws down the throats of frustrated business leaders.

26th December 2024

34 Trees

○→◇
↓
□←○

When in doubt, branch out: The science of Decision Trees

A decision tree is a visual and analytical decision support tool used to map out possible outcomes, costs, and benefits of various choices. It helps in evaluating different courses of action by considering the potential consequences, including risks and rewards.

In A Level Business, decision trees are used to simplify complex decision-making processes, making it easier to analyse and compare the outcomes of different options.

In real-world AI systems, they are used to determine next steps, and 'best next action', by using probability factors applied to possible outcomes.

Decision trees provide a structured and interpretable way of modelling decision-making processes, where a problem is split into a tree-like structure of decisions and their possible consequences, including chance event outcomes, resource costs, and personal or social welfare.

Steps in AI algorithms

So how do these AI system work? There is a four step process, as follows.

1. Data Splitting: Decision trees split data into subsets based on the value of input features. Each internal node represents a test on an attribute, each branch represents the outcome of the test, and each leaf node represents a class label (decision taken after computing all attributes).
2. Partitioning: The process starts with the entire dataset. The algorithm selects the feature that best splits the data into common and distinct groups.
3. Tree Building: The algorithm continues splitting each subset until the stopping criterion is met. Criteria can include a maximum depth of the tree, minimum number of samples per leaf, or until no further improvement can be made.
4. Prediction: For making predictions, the input data travels from the root of the tree to a leaf node. The class or value at the leaf node is the prediction of the model.

Real life examples

Diagnosing diseases. A decision tree can be used to classify patients into different categories of diseases based on symptoms and medical history. Each node in the tree represents a medical test or symptom, and branches represent possible outcomes (e.g., 'fever' could lead to branches for 'high' and 'normal' temperature). The leaf nodes represent diagnoses (e.g., 'flu,' 'cold,' 'COVID-19').

Predicting house prices. A decision tree can predict the price of a house based on attributes like location, number of bedrooms, square footage, recent market activity in the area, national economic measures and other social trends. The tree splits the data into smaller regions where houses are similar in value. The leaf nodes represent the predicted price.

Credit scoring. Banks use *random forests* to predict the likelihood of a customer defaulting on a loan. Each tree might use different subsets of customer data (e.g., credit history, income, employment status, buying behaviour, and patterns of loan repayment) to make predictions. The ensemble approach increases accuracy and robustness.

A school assignment

Decision trees provide a clear and interpretable way to make decisions based on data, which is essential for many AI applications. By partitioning data, they can handle complex decision-making processes.

I asked an A Level class to use a decision tree to determine whether the school should invest in iPads for all students, and move away from paper based work, folders and assignments.

The two option nodes were: (1) 'Invest in iPads' and (2) 'Do nothing'.

Setting out the capital costs of hardware and software investment, training and implementation, the students then added on-going service, maintenance and upgrade costs. All in, this was around £600,000. They then analysed benefits (savings on paper, saving on time, improved engagement, better student results, faster assignment turnarounds, and faster marking) and tried to quantify them. This was difficult. Then they added any qualitative benefits, such as a positive environmental sustainability impact. They quantified around £160,000 in on-going benefits. This was considered high and a probability of success of 0.3 was applied.

They added another investment approval technique - *Payback Period*. This was around 4 years.

They then compared this with option (2), the costs and benefits of doing nothing.

In conclusion, due to the high initial investment, whilst introducing iPads could be beneficial in the long run - due to annual cost savings on paper, improved student performance, and enhanced learning experiences - the uncertainty around the outcomes and success probability, coupled with a range of estimates for benefits, meant that the school should not invest in iPads for students and teachers. The payback period was also considered beyond the investment criteria set out by the financial policies of the Trust.

29th December 2024

VIII – Work

Quint: *You got city hands, Mr Hooper. Been countin' money all your life.*

Hooper: *Hey! I don't need this. I don't need this working class hero crap.*

– *Jaws*

35 Road

China's Belt and Road Initiative

As recently as 2005, the British economy was larger than the Chinese economy. Now China's economy is seven times larger. In 2006 it overtook Germany. In 2007 it overtook Japan.

Modern History

Since 2013, China has been responsible for 40% of all global *growth*. The EU has been 9% of global growth, and the US is at 22%.

China represents 20% of the global economy, and has had a 10% annual growth rate over the last 30 years. In the UK, we'd be delighted with 2% growth.

China is the: (i) largest manufacturing economy in the world, (ii) largest exporter of goods, (iii) fastest growing consumer market, (iv) second largest importer of goods, (v) largest recipient of Foreign Direct Investment (FDI is when overseas firms invest in factories, shops, warehouses, land). It has a growing middle class, numbering 400m.

When Deng Xiaoping became China's leader in 1979, it was a poor country. He opened up the Chinese economy to market forces and lifted hundreds of millions of people out of extreme poverty. Extreme poverty has a UN definition - living on less than $2 a day.

The current premier, Xi Jinping, has a new mission and vision, to connect the world through trade routes called the *Belt and Road Initiative*. It's a massive infrastructure investment that covers 155 countries. Roads, railways, bridges, dams, ports. In Indonesia, a rail link that was a 3 hour journey, was cut down to 45 minutes.

The United States does not offer a competing vision.

China not only finances and builds these connection routes, but it's also maintaining and running them. In Kenya, the train line between Mombasa and Nairobi has Chinese employees running the service.

China is well positioned for the energy transition. It dominates the production of wind turbines, solar panels and the processing of cobalt and lithium for our smartphone and electric-vehicle batteries.

Contrasting visions

The USA spent and eye-watering $3.7 trillion on the interventions in Iraq and Afghanistan, and achieved next to nothing. Afghanistan went from the Taliban to a US occupation and - $1.5 trillion later - back to the Taliban.

That same total amount, $3.7 trillion, is roughly the same that China has spent on the *Belt and Road Initiative*. The *World Bank* estimates that this initiative will boost trade flows in the 155 participating countries by 4%, cut the cost of trade by 2%, and grow the GDP of those countries by between 2% to 4%. We are not just talking about Africa and Asia – this includes Spain and Ireland.

Critics call this 'debt-trap diplomacy' and neo-colonialism. But for China, projecting growth and power, this project has been a success.

Challenges

The question is whether the participating countries can service their debt. The risk for China is not being repaid for these assets.

Much of this drive has been fuelled by a property boom, but this has slowed down after Covid. There are now $80 billion worth of unfinished apartments. One company alone, Evergrande, has built 300,000 homes in the last year, but is running into financial trouble and has 720,000 already paid-for homes still to build. This has the feel of the US sub-prime mortgage disaster that led to the 2008 financial crash.

The speed of China's development risks making the financing and maintenance costs unaffordable.

Japan was in this position before. In the 1980s, it was leading in technology, and was poised to become a world power. Japan hit a buffer due to its debt and its demographic changes – ageing population and low birth rate. Japan was unable to close the deal on its global ambitions. China is possibly heading for this same sclerosis.

14th December 2023

36 Income

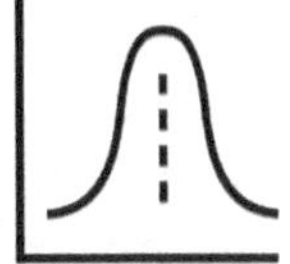

The myth of worsening income inequality

It is a truth universally acknowledged that income inequality has become worse over the past 50 years. Or so we thought. A new study shows that this much-quoted research is rife with errors and deeply flawed in its methodology.

Democrat senator Bernie Sanders says income inequality is the 'great moral, economic, and political issue of our time.'

But what if this was based on a series of mistakes?

That's the radical implication of a ground-breaking new study published in the *Journal of Political Economy,* from the *University of Chicago*. Authors Gerald Auten and David Splinter find that, when accurately measured, 'income inequality' has actually barely changed since 1962.

Research from writer Thomas Piketty has driven most of the media coverage and public discussion over income inequality. His research looked at US income-tax returns and reported massive increases in the share of income being earned by the top 1 percent, compared with no change for the bottom half of earners. But it turns out that Piketty's research is full of errors and has a flawed methodology.

Piketty's widely reported 2003 study found that since 1962 the income share earned by the top 1 percent more than doubled. It reached this conclusion by looking at individual income-tax returns.

However, income-tax returns don't account for government transfers, such as welfare and benefits programmes, nor do they account for non-taxable job benefits such as health insurance and retirement plans. They also fail to capture a significant portion of national income that doesn't show up on individual income-tax returns.

As a result, this gives a 'distorted view of income inequality levels and trends', say Auten and Splinter.

Their own analysis, which adjusts for these issues and examines after-tax, after-transfers income levels – the reality that people actually experience – finds very different results. Rather than doubling, they find that the share of income earned by the top 1 percent increased only 0.2 percentage points since 1962.

They also find that the supposed stagnation plaguing the bottom half of earners no longer exists once you look at post-tax, post-welfare data. Auten and Splinter report: 'Instead of real per capita incomes of the bottom half of the distribution appearing unchanged since 1979, we find that after taxes and transfers they *increased by two-thirds*.'

Unfortunately, their research is unlikely to receive the attention that Piketty's did because it's not useful for ideological progressives. The narrative of soaring inequality helps progressive media activists make the case for the radical redistribution of wealth advocated by Senator Bernie Sanders, and others.

'Piketty made a habit of pushing out deeply suspect statistical claims about rising inequality by taking them to ideologically friendly reporters,' says economic historian Phil Magness. 'Journalists use Piketty's stats to stoke a political narrative about chronic inequality. They then make the case for tax increases to combat the supposed problem.'

'Meanwhile, more-accurate and methodical inequality metrics take years to produce,' he concluded. 'Most other measures show a modest change in inequality at best.'

'The conclusion from the literature is that we don't have a good estimate of what has happened to inequality,' economist Brian Albrecht, who has analysed the research in this area. 'The problem is that the most sensational number gets the headlines. So if ten economics papers find numbers between zero change and doubling, the media will focus on the doubling result.'

So, the real lesson from this new research is not that income inequality is a non-issue. It is that statistics which suit one side's ideological narrative need a healthy dose of scepticism.

18th April 2024

37 Teaching VI

The pleasures of learning and knowing

'Τι δε μοι πλέον έσται ταύτα μαθόντι;'
Και ο Ευκλείδης τον παίδα καλέσας – 'δος αυτώ τριώβολον, επειδή δει αυτώ εξ ων μανθάνει κερδαίνειν.'

A geometry student of Euclid, when he had learnt the first theorem asked Euclid, 'But what advantage shall I get by learning these things?'
Euclid called his slave and said, 'Give him threepence, since he needs to make a profit out of what he learns.'

– Euclid, Extracts II, 31, 114

This is a common student question: 'Sir, will we ever need to use this?'

Quadratic equations, Pythagoras, congruent triangles, square roots. Who has used any of these in adult life? Scientists perhaps. Engineers maybe. Architects at a stretch.

I have tried several times to give answers to students who ask this question. But none of mine have been as good as the original answer, above, given by the father of geometry, Euclid, in Athens, in 300 BC.

That was the original *'Here's 20p. Go and call someone who cares.'* (For those who remember phone-boxes before mobile phones).

Education is valuable for personal and societal development, even when knowledge may not always be directly applied.

1. *Cultivation of critical thinking:* Education develops problem-solving skills, enabling individuals to evaluate information, make informed decisions, and navigate complex situations in life.
2. *Broadening horizons:* Education exposes students to a wide range of ideas and cultures, fostering open-mindedness and cultural awareness. It helps individuals appreciate diversity and develop empathy.
3. *Personal growth:* Education contributes to personal growth and self-discovery. It empowers individuals to explore their interests, talents, and passions, nurturing their sense of self-worth and identity.
4. *Effective communication:* Education improves writing, speaking, and listening, in order to build relationships, resolve conflicts, and convey ideas.
5. *Citizenship and civic engagement:* Education equips individuals with an understanding of societal issues and politics. Informed citizens are more likely to engage in civic activities and contribute to their communities.
6. *Lifelong learning:* Education instils a love for learning and the ability to adapt to new challenges throughout life, promoting continuous personal and professional development.

7. *Health literacy:* Education enables individuals to make informed decisions about their well-being and navigate the healthcare system effectively.
8. *Cultural preservation:* Education helps to preserve cultural heritage and traditions by passing down customs and languages to future generations.
9. *Critical consumption of information:* Education helps individuals sift through vast amounts of data, discern credible sources from misinformation, and become responsible consumers of information.
10. *Fulfilment and enrichment:* Knowledge itself is intrinsically valuable, enriching individuals' lives by providing a deeper understanding of the world, its complexities and beauty. Learning can bring fulfilment and purpose.

'Two households ...'

I once had to cover a Music lesson. The cover work said, *'Play the film 'West Side Story'. Students to describe a song using musical terms.'*

I skipped through the movie and played them four songs. Then I played them all again. They wrote their musical terms. Then I asked them to vote for their favourite song.

These were the scores: –

- *Maria* 0
- *America* 0
- *Gee, Officer Krupke* 22
- *I Feel Pretty* 0

Then we had ten minutes left. Time to show off. I drew up on the board two columns and called one Romeo and the other Juliet and told the class that *West Side Story* was an adaptation of Shakespeare's play.

Underneath each column I wrote Capulets v. Montagues, Sharks v. Jets, Tony and Maria. I wasn't sure under which columns the family and gang names should go, but it didn't matter. I guess that's the point. It doesn't matter which tribe you belong to.

9th November 2023

38 Teaching VII

Bridging educational attainment gaps with AI

The education industry is freaking out about AI. Some institutions have imposed a blanket ban on *ChatGPT*. To complete an assignment using AI is considered *plagiarism.*

To enforce this rule, academies turn to AI detectors, which use statistical patterns to identify texts produced by machines. These are so unreliable that *OpenAI*, the creator of *ChatGPT*, pulled its own detection product due to inaccuracy.

Students who learn how to use AI will have an advantage over those who choose not to.

American academic Ethan Zuckerman estimates that a third of his students have disclosed their use of AI. Their work was not measurably better or worse than that of students who have not disclosed use of AI, which isn't all that surprising.

A new study from a team of business school professors working with *Boston Consulting Group* found that AI had a levelling effect on many tasks, with the bottom performers significantly enhancing their output, and top performers improving only a little.

I encourage students to use AI - but to then shape, polish, re-write and apply the content to their knowledge and sprinkle it with their own insights and examples. AI is superb at experimentation - for example using *ChatGPT* as a brainstorming partner. In my experience, AI engines give competent but uninspiring answers.

The surprising and exciting ideas in essay homework, are more likely to have come from the students themselves.

Students often express concerns about becoming too dependent on technology. We have all learnt to use and rely on Sat-Nav. I can't navigate unfamiliar places the way our parents did, from landmarks and memory. It's possible that students will end up similarly dependent on AI. Yet we have no desire to return to navigation using paper maps.

Computer programming students using generative AI as a *'co-pilot'*, say it helps automate the tedious and repetitive parts of writing code. These students are vastly more productive than those writing code entirely by hand. This is because they have good coding skills to start with and can detect when their AI co-pilot makes errors.

The problem is that the AI co-pilots can pass most assignments for an introductory course, meaning that we might not be able to train competent programmers in the first place, as beginners will be able to avoid the frustrating and challenging work of learning to code that is a necessary part of developing expertise.

We should be less worried about students gaming the system than about losing their trust. Students are most concerned about being falsely accused of using AI, particularly when teachers use pattern and plagiarism detectors. Some even report receiving failing grades in classes for using AI on assignments that they insist were completed manually.

It is sometimes helpful to write in a text editor like *Google Docs*, which can maintain snapshots of a document as it is written, showing that it was not cut and pasted from AI.

So, as hundreds of task forces are set up on generative AI, we should be making the case that we must not discourage its use, but that we should approach teaching from a position of collaborative discovery, trust, and kindness rather than distrust.

In the next few years, every profession will need to figure out what it means to use AI effectively and ethically. Those whose job it is to prepare students for work in this new world, that we're figuring out together in real time, should not be penalising them, when it's our methods of academic evaluation that need to change.

21st March 2024

39 Norway

Norway's Sovereign Wealth Fund

'This Earth was made a common treasury for everyone to share,
All things in common, all people one.'
— Leon Rosselson, *The World Turned Upside Down*

Of the people, for the people

When countries discover oil and gas reserves on their land or within their territorial waters, it can be as much of a curse as it is a blessing.

Corruption, vested interests, oligarchical greed and inequitable distribution of the fruits, all create an environment that rewards the wrong behaviours. This has happened countless times in kleptocratic states like Venezuela, Azerbaijan and Angola.

In some cases, however, the wealth is invested to 'future-proof' the economy against the depletion of the oil. Saudi Arabia, for example, is investing in digital cities, agricultural innovation, renewable resources, engineering technology, and is sponsoring sports worldwide, such as Formula 1, golf and football.

Norway is one shining beacon of light that is demonstrating world class custodianship of its 'commons'.

The '*commons*' is a phrase that dates from the Magna Carta of 1215, and refers to the shared resources held in common for community use and benefit - land, water, air and the natural resources within them. A 'crisis of the commons' is sometimes used to describe the negative effects of carving up these resources for private, and often corporate, benefit, when they are considered to be *public goods*.

Norway is an oil-rich state, with massive oil and gas reserves, and fifty years' experience in the industry. It is the third largest exporter of natural gas in the world - after the USA and Qatar - and the 9th largest crude oil exporter.

The Norwegian *Statens pensjonsfond* comprises sovereign wealth funds owned by the government of Norway. Its *Oil Fund,* was established in 1990 to invest the surplus revenues of the Norwegian petroleum sector. It has over $1.2 trillion in assets and holds 1.4% of all the world's listed companies. It is one of the world's largest sovereign wealth funds, investing in over 9,000 companies across 70 countries.

The fund is worth about $250,000 per Norwegian citizen. Norway only has a population of 5.4 million. The fund holds portfolios of real estate and fixed-income investments.

As a result of the large size of the fund, it has become a hot political issue, dominated by whether the country should use more of the petroleum revenues for the state budget instead of saving the funds for the future.

Norway set up an *Ethical council* to consider the investments of the fund. The Ministry of Finance then announced that 17 tobacco companies would be excluded from the fund. The total divestment from these companies was $2 billion - the largest ever known ethical led divestment.

Not so secret recipe

Norway regularly features very high up in global tables of the world's happiest, wealthiest, healthiest and most equal societies.

Norway has strong social cohesion, with a deep-rooted sense of community and mutual trust. This is underpinned by transparency, a strong legal framework, and low corruption.

The country's progressive taxation system redistributes wealth effectively, reducing income disparities and fosters collective responsibility.

This leads to robust public services. Often referred to as the *Nordic Model,* this provides its citizens with a safety net that includes free healthcare, education, and generous pensions.

After gaining independence from Sweden in 1905, Norway embraced democratic principles. It emphasises education, ensuring that its population is well-equipped to participate in a modern economy.

Norwegians have a deep connection to nature, which influences both their quality of life and their approach to sustainability. The country is a leader in renewable energy, particularly hydropower. This respect for nature is also reflected in the high value placed on outdoor activities, contributing to the well-being of its citizens.

16th August 2024

40 Hazards

Moral hazards, moral judgments: Financial sector immunity

'Austerity is the idea that the worldwide financial crash of 2008 was caused by Wolverhampton having too many libraries.'
— Alexei Sayle

Why is it that it's always the wealthy bankers that get the bailouts, and it's the poor who get the austerity?

This dynamic is a reflection of systemic inequalities in economic and political systems. Here are some reasons why this tends to happen.

Systemically important

Banks and financial institutions are considered the backbone of the economy. Governments believe their collapse would trigger widespread economic devastation, including mass unemployment and the loss of savings. This leads to a 'too big to fail' mentality, where bailouts are justified to prevent broader harm.

In contrast, low-income households are not viewed as directly vital to the economy, despite their roles as consumers and workers.

Political influence

Wealthy bankers and financial elites have significant lobbying power and political connections. They can influence policies to protect their interests, often through campaign contributions and behind-the-scenes negotiations.

Poor and working-class people generally lack such direct access to policymakers, leading to their needs being deprioritised. We should, however, also avoid the tendency to lump together people who are in reality very distinct and varied groups.

Economic ideology

Modern economic policies often prioritise market stability and investor confidence. This means financial institutions are bailed out to maintain global economic credibility, while austerity is imposed on the public to reduce deficits and reassure markets.

Austerity disproportionately affects those in most need of public services, as cuts in wages and benefits hit them hardest.

Asymmetry of accountability

When banks collapse, the blame is often diffused or shifted onto 'market conditions.' This leads to public bailouts with minimal repercussions for the bankers themselves.

Those in regular jobs are held to stricter standards. Austerity measures often come with rhetoric blaming the public for overspending or relying too much on social safety nets.

Moral hazard vs. moral judgment

Governments justify bailouts for banks to avoid systemic risks but impose austerity on the poor under the guise of promoting fiscal discipline.

Wealthy elites benefit from a *moral hazard* where their risky behaviour is subsidised, while the poor face *moral judgment,* with their struggles framed as personal failings rather than systemic issues.

The disparity in treatment stems from structural imbalances of power, economic ideology, and the framing of crises. Addressing this inequality would require a shift in political priorities, greater regulation of financial elites, and stronger advocacy for the needs of marginalised populations.

Legacy

The 2008-2009 financial crisis had devastating effects on employment and housing in both the United States and Europe.

In the United States, approximately 8.7 million jobs were lost during the Great Recession, doubling the unemployment rate. Millions of Americans faced debt default (what Americans call *foreclosure*), leading to a significant loss of homes.

In Europe, the crisis led to substantial job losses across European countries, with unemployment rates soaring, particularly in nations like Spain and Greece. Many European households experienced housing instability, with increased default on loans and evictions, especially in countries severely affected by the crisis.

Despite these widespread hardships, many bankers retained their high-paying positions and continued to engage in risky financial strategies.

Regulatory capture

Another root cause of the problem, is the movement of individuals between roles as regulators and executive positions within the industries they oversee - often creating conflicts of interest. This 'revolving door' can lead to regulatory decisions that favour industry interests over public welfare.

Financial institutions often exert significant influence over regulatory bodies through lobbying efforts, campaign contributions, and other means. This influence can result in regulations that are more favourable to the industry, sometimes at the expense of the interest of broader society.

These factors contribute to a regulatory environment where the interests of powerful financial entities are prioritised, often leading to adverse outcomes for the general population, particularly during economic downturns.

3rd January 2025

41 Barbershops

Cutting corners: The shady barbershop boom

In recent years, there has been growing concern about the noticeable number of barbershops across the UK - including areas like Coventry, Southall, Hayes and Greenford - with many being investigated for potentially operating as fronts for criminal activities such as money laundering, drug trafficking, and modern slavery.

The surge in numbers, with over 17,000 barbershops reported nationwide, has raised suspicions about the legitimacy of some businesses, especially those that operate as cash-only establishments or offer suspiciously low-priced services.

The shops have high-end equipment and lighting, expensive barber's chairs and flooring ... and surprisingly few customers.

Law enforcement and trafficking experts have highlighted specific warning signs, such as frequent staff turnover, poor working conditions, and cash-only operations, which can indicate exploitation or criminal ties.

Some cases have also linked barbershops to human trafficking networks, with workers being victims of modern slavery. These concerns align with broader patterns seen in other industries like car washes and nail salons, which have also been identified as vulnerable to abuse by criminal organisations.

MPs and local authorities have called for closer scrutiny, particularly in regions like Coventry, where the density of barbershops on some streets seems disproportionate.

The Member of Parliament of Prestatyn, in Wales, Gareth Davies, said the only businesses doing well in the retail sector were barbers, car washes, and vape shops.

'It's funny,' said Davies, 'that the only businesses on the average Welsh high street that appear to be thriving unimpeded by the Welsh government these days are pop-up barber shops, unsightly vaping and e-cig outlets, and cash-only hand car washes, amongst other money laundering fronts.

'Prestatyn High Street had two barber shops 15 years ago, but there are a dozen now, all of a similar theme.'

One indication of malpractice is when a customer arrives, and a tired or dishevelled barber comes downstairs to start working on them. Other warning signs include: the business only takes cash payments, staff appear to live on the premises, look exhausted and are distant from management. The number of people who work at a barbers are also a cause for concern.

Candy

This close scrutiny follows on from the fraud investigation into the US-style candy shops on Oxford Street, which had hidden a million pounds worth of counterfeit goods in 2022.

American candy stores up and down one of Europe's busiest shopping roads have been caught with huge amounts of counterfeit of illegal goods over the last six months. There are 30 stores along the Oxford Street being investigated for failing to pay £8 million in business rates.

Westminster City Council seized £474,000 worth of counterfeit goods in 2024 - including 2,000 counterfeit Wonka Bars, 2,800 disposable vapes, 220 toys with no safety labels, and 1,400 counterfeit phone covers.

The seized vapes, which were both counterfeit and had excessive nicotine levels, also came with tank sizes larger than the permitted amount by the government's regulatory agency.

Organisations like Companies House (where companies are registered) and HMRC (which collects taxes) have struggled to take action, and often don't have the resources or the legal mandate to investigate.

A two-year police investigation into the forced labour of Vietnamese teenagers at *Deluxe Nails* in Bath and *Gorgeous Nails* in Burton-on-Trent resulted in the conviction of three people, Thu Huong Nguyen (known as Jenny), Viet Hoang Nguyen (Ken) and Giang Huong Tran (Susan).

The Home Office estimates as many as 13,000 people in the UK could be affected by modern slavery. Separate research from *Freedom United*, which includes new forms of slavery such as child drug-runners, suggests this number could, in fact, be as high as 136,000.

8th December 2024

IX – Mathematics

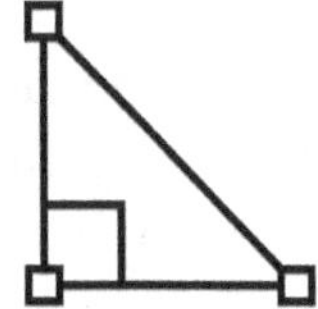

'If I were again beginning my studies, I would follow the advice of Plato and start with mathematics.'

– Galileo

42 Fibonacci II

Fibonacci numbers and humpbacks

The Fibonacci sequence is a series of numbers where each term is the sum of the two preceding ones, typically starting with 0 and 1. So the sequence goes: 0, 1, 1, 2, 3, 5, 8, 13, 21, 34, and so on. This sequence exhibits a spiral pattern when plotted graphically. It was discovered over 800 years ago by Leonardo Fibonacci, in 1202, when he observed the mating habits and offspring of rabbits.

In nature, the Fibonacci sequence is seen in the arrangement of leaves on a stem, the spirals of sea-shells, and the petals of flowers. For example, the number of petals on a flower often corresponds to a Fibonacci number, such as lilies with three petals, buttercups with five, and daisies with 34, which are Fibonacci numbers. Similarly, the spiral patterns seen in sunflower heads, pine-cones, and the shells of snails follow Fibonacci sequences.

The importance of the Fibonacci sequence in nature lies in its role in optimising efficiency and maximising space. By following these mathematical patterns, plants arrange their leaves and petals to maximise exposure to sunlight and airflow, while minimising competition for resources. Likewise, the spiral growth patterns in shells and tree branches allow organisms to efficiently pack genetic material and physical structures in a compact and aesthetically pleasing manner.

In art, the Fibonacci sequence has been a source of inspiration for centuries, influencing the works of artists, architects, and designers. It is used to create compositions that are visually appealing and harmonious. The Parthenon in Athens and the pyramids of Egypt adhere to Fibonacci ratios, creating balance and symmetry that are pleasing to the eye.

Artists incorporate Fibonacci ratios into their compositions to guide the viewer's gaze and create a sense of movement and rhythm. Paintings such as Leonardo da Vinci's 'The Last Supper' and Salvador Dali's 'The Sacrament of the Last Supper' contain Fibonacci sequences, enhancing their aesthetic appeal and symbolic significance.

Humpback whales, with their majestic presence and intricate behaviours, have fascinated scientists with their creation of Fibonacci patterns in the ocean. These patterns, characterised by spirals and curves of the Fibonacci sequence, are visually stunning but also serve important purposes for the whales.

One of the primary reasons humpback whales create Fibonacci patterns is for navigation and hunting. These patterns are often observed during feeding parties, where groups of whales work together to entice and capture schools of fish. By swimming in synchronised patterns that resemble Fibonacci spirals, the whales effectively herd their prey into concentrated areas, making it easier to feed. This activity demonstrates the whales' intelligence and cooperation, using mathematical principles to enhance their hunting success.

Additionally, Fibonacci patterns may play a role in communication among humpback whales. These intricate designs serve as visual signals about the location of food, potential threats, or mating opportunities. Through the use of Fibonacci patterns, humpback whales communicate complex messages to coordinate their activities and ensure the survival of their pod.

Nature often favours patterns and structures that minimise energy expenditure, and Fibonacci sequences are a prime example of this. By following these mathematical patterns, humpback whales optimise their movements, streamline their hunting efforts, conserve energy and maximise their chances of survival and mating success.

Furthermore, the creation of Fibonacci patterns by whales may have evolutionary roots. Whales that exhibit Fibonacci sequence behaviour gain competitive advantage, leading to the perpetuation of these traits through natural selection. As a result, the ability to create Fibonacci patterns could be an adaptive trait that has been honed over generations.

13th June 2024

43 Widows

An untold story of numbers

A new and evolving branch of mathematics was created 150 years ago to handle some complicated problems in society. We call it statistics.

In 1744, two priests in Scotland, Alexander Webster and Robert Wallace, set up a life insurance fund that would look after the widows and orphans of dead clergymen.

They proposed that each minister would pay a small proportion of his income into the fund which would invest the money. If the minister died, his widow would receive an income from the fund's profits, that would allow her to live comfortably for the rest of her life.

To determine how much the ministers had to pay, so that the fund could fulfil its commitments, Webster and Wallace had to predict how many ministers would die each year, how many widows and orphans they would leave behind, and by how many years the widows would outlive their husbands.

Being Scots, Webster and Wallace were practical chaps. They contacted a Professor of Mathematics from the University of Edinburgh, Colin Maclaurin.

The three of them collected data on the ages at which people died, and used these to calculate how many ministers were likely to pass away in any given year. Their work was founded on several recent breakthroughs in the fields of statistics and probability. One of these was Jacob Bernoulli's *Law of Large Numbers*.

They had ready-made data that they could use. Actuarial tables published fifty years earlier proved useful. These tables made it possible to see that a twenty year old person had a one in one hundred chance of dying in a given year, but a fifty year old person has a one in thirty-nine chance.

Processing these numbers, Webster and Wallace concluded that, on average, there would be 930 living Scottish Presbyterian ministers at any given moment. And an average of 27 ministers would die each year, 18 of whom would be survived by widows. Five of those who did not leave widows would leave orphaned children. And two of those survived by widows would also be outlived by children from previous marriages who had not yet reached the age of 16.

They further computed how much time was likely to go by before the widow's death or re-marriage; in both these eventualities payment of the pension would cease.

These figures enabled Webster and Wallace to determine how much money the ministers who joined their fund had to pay in order to provide for their loved ones.

By contributing two pounds, twelve shillings and tuppence a year, a minister could guarantee that his widowed wife would receive at least ten pounds a year. A substantial sum in those days.

According to their calculations, they estimated that by the year 1765, the *Fund for a Provision of the Widows and*

Children of the Ministers of the Church of Scotland would have £58,348.

Their calculations proved amazingly accurate. Twenty years later, when the year 1765 arrived, the fund stood at £58,347. Just one pound less than the prediction.

Today, Webster and Wallace's fund, known simply at *Scottish Widows,* is one of the largest pension and insurance companies in the world, with assets worth £100 billion. It insures not only Scottish widows, but anyone willing to buy its policies.

Probability calculations such as those used by the two ministers became the foundation of actuarial science, which is central to the pension and insurance business, but also to demography.

Demography was founded by another clergyman, the Anglican Robert Malthus. In turn, Charles Darwin used demography and probability for his theory of evolution.

25th April 2024

44 Racist

Numbers don't lie, but do they discriminate?

A controversial belief, lacking substantial evidence, has recently gained traction in some American and British universities. There have been claims that mathematics can perpetuate biases and that traditional teaching methods uphold oppressive structures—even suggesting that mathematics itself is racist.

This perspective posits that mathematics, as traditionally taught, can reinforce inequalities by emphasising a narrow set of skills or by being insufficiently inclusive of diverse approaches to problem-solving.

This is not an exaggeration. One encounters elements of this ideology when training as a mathematics teacher.

Claims

The first claim argues that emphasising 'correct answers' in mathematics reinforces elitism and systemic inequality. Some argue that focusing on accuracy privileges certain types of knowledge, often labelled as 'Western' or 'white' knowledge, which allegedly marginalises other cultural perspectives.

The second claim suggests that promoting individual achievements and competition in mathematics fosters inequality by prioritising individualism over community and collaborative learning.

Finally, traditional grading practices in mathematics are accused of perpetuating racial bias. Critics argue that standardised assessments may fail to account for cultural or socioeconomic differences among students, contributing to racial disparities.

Rebuttals

Emphasising correct answers: Focusing on correct answers is not about perpetuating elitism but about ensuring competency in essential skills. Research consistently shows that mathematics proficiency correlates with improved economic and life outcomes across all demographics. For instance, a 2020 study by the *National Bureau of Economic Research* found that mathematics achievement in school significantly increases earnings and reduces the likelihood of poverty in adulthood across racial and ethnic groups.

Mastery of correct answers isn't a cultural preference; it's a reliable predictor of personal and professional success.

Competition and individual achievement: Competition in mathematics has been shown to improve motivation and outcomes. Data from the *Programme for International Student Assessment* (PISA) reveals that countries with a strong emphasis on competition and achievement in mathematics – such as China, Japan, South Korea, Singapore, Israel, and Finland – consistently outperform those that downplay competition. These educational systems foster accomplishment and resilience, translating into real-world skills.

Moreover, competition does not inherently disadvantage any demographic. When supported by equitable access to resources, competition can be a powerful tool for engagement and excellence.

Standardised assessments: Transparent and standardised assessments can mitigate bias by providing objective, consistent benchmarks for all students. Research by *Harvard's Center for Education Policy Research* (CEPR) found that standardised mathematics assessments reduced instances of subjective grading, which is often influenced by implicit biases. Clear and consistent grading practices also enable teachers to identify areas where students need targeted support, helping to close achievement gaps without discarding objective standards.

Immunity of mathematics

Mathematics is rooted in objective logic and proof, relying on provable truths that are independent of cultural or ideological influence. Two plus two equals four, irrespective of the social context.

Fields like engineering, physics, and economics depend on precise calculations and predictable outcomes – practical applications that highlight mathematics as a universal language. These fields underscore the subject's relevance and applicability across diverse cultural settings, leaving little room for ideological reinterpretation.

Evidence consistently shows that focusing on correct answers, fostering achievement, and using standardised assessments provide equitable benefits and opportunities across all student demographics. These practices are fundamental to building fair and effective education systems, and are not barriers to equality.

When you encounter phrases like 'Critical Theory' or 'decolonising the curriculum,' challenge these ideas. While often well-intentioned, they risk introducing divisive ideologies into education, promoting resentment rather than meaningful progress.

Competence, not power

The world's progress has been driven by competence, not by power. This principle is evident in both animal behaviour and human societal structures.

Studies by primatologist Frans de Waal of chimpanzee troops and gorilla bands reveal that when a leader becomes aggressive, selfish, or tyrannical, social cohesion deteriorates. Such leaders often lose the group's loyalty, and coalitions form to overthrow them. Successful leaders in these groups balance dominance with reciprocal behaviours, such as sharing resources and offering protection. When leaders fail to act benevolently, they are typically replaced by individuals who better balance strength with cooperation.

Sustainable hierarchies – whether in the animal kingdom or human societies – depend on competence and mutual benefit, not oppression or fear.

Mathematics, grounded in objective logic and universal truths, remains one of the most effective tools for empowering individuals and fostering social progress. By upholding evidence-based practices in mathematics education, we can ensure equitable opportunities for all students, resisting divisive ideologies that seek to undermine its foundations.

21st December 2024

45 Harmony

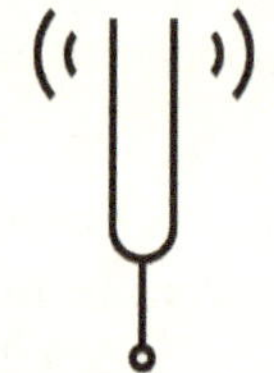

The marriage of geometry and melody: Musical maths from Pythagoras to Glass

Hellenistic roots

Pythagoras, the ancient Greek mathematician, made significant contributions in many fields including politics, cosmology, and philosophy. One of his lesser-known interests was music. He developed music theory and the understanding of harmony.

Pythagoras was born in 570 BCE on the Greek island of Samos. One of the founders of Western mathematics, his work with numbers and geometric shapes is still taught in schools today.

Pythagoras discovered the mathematical relationships underlying musical intervals. He noticed that the sounds produced by plucking strings of varying lengths on a musical instrument followed a pattern. By plucking a string that was half the length of another, he observed that the resulting note was eight scale degrees higher – one octave.

This observation led to the concept of octave equivalence, where notes with frequencies in a 2:1 ratio are perceived as being harmonically related.

He further discovered that the division of a string into specific proportions created measurable intervals, such as the perfect fifth (a 3:2 ratio) and the perfect fourth (a 4:3 ratio). These findings laid the foundation for Western music theory, and Western tuning systems, as they revealed the fundamental mathematical relationships that underly musical harmony. (Fifths and octaves are the intervals or gaps between notes. A jump from a C to a G moves the scale higher by five degrees).

Plato, a student of Pythagoras' followers, was deeply inspired by these mathematical approaches to music. In his work *The Republic,* Plato discussed the importance of music in education and its power to shape the character of individuals and society.

Baroque

There have been numerous academic studies on the relationship between mathematics and the music of Johann Sebastian Bach (1685 - 1750). Researchers have identified various mathematical patterns, such as symmetry, proportion, and numerical sequences within Bach's music, suggesting a deliberate integration of mathematical principles in his compositions.

Bach's ability to write in highly structured forms highlights a systematic approach that mirrors arithmetic logic. The *Well-Tempered Clavier,* for instance, explores all major and minor keys, showing a geometric exploration of harmony.

A *Bach chorale* refers to a harmonised version of a Lutheran hymn tune, typically written for four voices:

soprano, alto, tenor, and bass. Bach composed hundreds of chorales, often as part of larger cantatas and passions, but many stand independently. The leading voices are crafted with smooth melodic motion and attention to harmonic progression.

Chorales exhibit structured, repeating patterns that lend themselves to analysis as dynamic systems, offering insights into stability and change in musical forms. Bach chorales are not just beautiful examples of music but also rich, structured data sets that illuminate the interplay between art and mathematics.

Bach's use of counterpoint, where multiple melodies are woven together in precise, interdependent relationships, is an illuminating example of how the mathematical concept of symmetry is reflected in how these melodies interact – moving in contrary motion or mirroring one another.

The fugue, a genre in which Bach excelled, showcases this mathematical rigour. The fugue is a musical composition where a theme is repeated or imitated. It is transformed through systematic processes, akin to solving an equation with multiple variables.

In Bach's hands, mathematics and music become an intertwined marriage of technical mastery and emotional richness. This is what makes his music enduringly powerful, bridging the worlds of abstract numbers and human experience.

Minimalism

In the modern era, *Music in Fifths* (1969) by Philip Glass is a direct example of Pythagoras's ratios. The title refers to the intervals of perfect fifths that dominate the composition. Glass builds melody and harmony almost entirely using these intervals.

Glass employs what he calls 'additive structure', where phrases gradually expand or contract by adding or subtracting a single note or beat. The steady, unrelenting tempo and incremental changes create a hypnotic, meditative effect. If the initial phrase has 4 notes, the next iteration might have 5 notes, then 6 notes, etc., forming a predictable growth pattern. This is conceptually similar to fractals or iterative functions in maths, where simple inputs generate intricate outcomes.

Glass's use of systematic processes mirrors algorithms in computer science. The incremental process embodies the mathematical concept of progression. Musicologist K. Robert Schwarz, in *Minimalists*, discusses Glass's use of 'reductive logic,' where arithmetic drives the evolution of his pieces.

The concept of polyrhythms involves layering rhythms with different time signatures (e.g., 3:2 or 4:3). These directly correspond to mathematical ratios. For example, Steve Reich's *Clapping Music* is based on phasing patterns, where one rhythm gradually shifts out of sync with another. This creates a mathematically predictable pattern of alignment and misalignment. Reich describes the mathematical basis of phasing in his book *Writings on Music*.

Fibonacci patterns

Studies have shown that some composers incorporate the *Golden Ratio*, a mathematical proportion often found in nature and art, into their compositions, lending support to the music's appeal and beauty.

The ratio is derived from the Fibonacci sequence of numbers, when the next term is determined by adding the previous two (0, 1, 1, 2, 3, 5, 8, 13, 21, 34 and so on). The pattern is seen throughout nature - petal patterns, veins on a leaf, branches of trees, and the circular designs on shells.

Scholars like David Yearsley in *Bach and the Meanings of Counterpoint* argue that Bach's work reflects mathematical rigour, but there is no direct proof of Fibonacci sequences in his music.

Composers such as Claude Debussy (1862 - 1918) and Béla Bartók (1881 - 1945) did directly use the golden ratio in their music. Bartók's *Music for Strings, Percussion, and Celesta* has structured sections based on Fibonacci numbers, such as the climax at the 0.618 point of the piece, approximating the golden ratio. Ernö Lendvai's book, *Béla Bartók: An Analysis of his Music,* provides detailed analysis of Fibonacci structures.

Iannis Xenakis (1922 - 2001) was one of the most innovative composers of the twentieth century. He applied mathematical processes and algorithmic influences on his compositions. His piece *Metastaseis* uses transformations like the Fibonacci sequence and probability theory to determine the placement of notes. Xenakis wrote about his methods in *Formalised Music: Thought and Mathematics in Composition*.

31st December 2024

46 Napoleon

Divide and Conquer: Napoleon's equations for success

Napoleon Bonaparte (1769–1821) was a French military leader and emperor who rose to prominence during the French Revolution. He established the Napoleonic Code, a legal framework that influenced modern civil law systems.

Napoleon expanded the French Empire through military campaigns, conquering much of Europe. He reformed education, centralised administration, and modernised the economy.

His strategic brilliance was evident in battles like Austerlitz and Jena, but his ambition led to overreach, including the disastrous invasion of Russia in 1812. After his defeat at Waterloo in 1815, he was exiled to Saint Helena. Napoleon remains a symbol of ambition and reform.

Napoleon's military campaigns are often lauded for their precise planning and reliance on mathematical calculations. His strategies revolved around the innovative use of logistics, troop movement, and timing to ensure that his armies could converge at critical points on the battlefield.

Centralised command, decentralised execution

Napoleon employed a centralised decision-making structure combined with flexible execution. He provided clear, precise orders to his marshals, using maps and mathematical calculations to determine the fastest and most efficient routes.

His corps system divided the army into semi-independent units capable of manoeuvring separately but able to unite quickly, often within a day's march. This system relied on detailed calculations of distance and time.

Geometric strategy

Napoleon used geometric principles to position his forces to maximum advantage. For example, he would organise his troops along an interior line, allowing shorter distances between units compared to enemies on an exterior line. This enabled him to concentrate forces more rapidly at decisive points.

Napoleon's armies often travelled in columns on parallel routes, spreading out across roads to avoid bottlenecks while converging precisely at a predetermined location. He calculated distances and marching speeds, factoring in terrain and weather.

A typical calculation might involve marching speeds of 15 miles per day for infantry and 25 miles per day for cavalry under normal conditions.

Napoleon's understanding of logistics allowed him to balance supply needs with speed. His forces lived off the land to minimise reliance on long supply lines, but he ensured depots were positioned along key routes, determined by precise calculations of consumption rates and delivery times.

Mathematics in artillery

As a trained artillery officer, Napoleon applied mathematical precision to the use of artillery. He calculated trajectories, ranges, and angles to maximise the effectiveness of bombardments, often softening enemy defences before major assaults.

Austerlitz (1805): At the Battle of Austerlitz, Napoleon used decoy movements and timing to trick the Austro-Russian forces into weakening their centre. His calculations allowed him to concentrate superior numbers at the decisive moment, resulting in a significant victory.

Jena-Auerstedt (1806): Napoleon's corps system allowed his forces to converge quickly on the Prussian army, overwhelming them in two closely coordinated battles.

The Ulm Campaign (1805): Napoleon's forces encircled and trapped the Austrian army at Ulm by precisely timing the convergence of multiple corps, forcing a surrender without a major battle.

Napoleon relied on a network of couriers to relay orders and updates, with each courier's speed calculated to ensure messages arrived on time. He sometimes used visual signals like semaphores, for faster communication.

While Napoleon's reliance on mathematical precision was revolutionary, it required immense discipline and effective execution by his subordinates. Failures in communication, unexpected terrain challenges, or delays often disrupted plans.

Napoleon's use of mathematics and precise planning influenced modern military strategy, especially in logistics, movement coordination, and the integration of different military branches.

26th December 2024

47 Irrational

The beauty in simplifying Surds

An irrational number is a number that cannot be expressed as a simple fraction (i.e., it cannot be written as a ratio of two whole numbers: a over b, where a and b are both whole numbers, and b is not zero). Unlike rational numbers, irrational numbers have non-terminating and non-repeating decimal expansions. In other words, after the decimal point they go on, literally, forever.

Examples of irrational numbers

$\sqrt{2}$: The square root of 2 is approximately 1.4142135… and it goes on without repeating. It's irrational because it cannot be exactly written as a fraction.

π (Pi): is approximately 3.14159265…, a famous irrational number that represents the ratio of a circle's circumference to its diameter. Its decimal expansion never ends or repeats.

e (Euler's Number): The constant *e*, roughly 2.7182818…, is another irrational number used in calculus, especially for exponential growth (accelerating), and natural logarithms (the '*undo*' button for exponential, for example, 'How many times do I need to double 2 to get to 8?').

Irrational numbers are essential in mathematics because they allow us to precisely describe many natural phenomena, geometric properties, and mathematical constants that cannot be accurately represented by fractions or whole numbers.

Surds

Surds are irrational numbers that can't be simplified into exact decimals or fractions, such as the square root of 2, (√2), or the square root of 3, (√3).

They have a unique elegance in mathematics because they allow us to work precisely with irrational values. Simplifying surds involves expressing these square roots or other roots in their simplest form, creating a balance between accuracy and simplicity.

For example, simplifying a surd like √50 to 5√2 shows how complex values can be represented with elegance and clarity. I can estimate that the square root of 50 is somewhere between the square root of 49 (which is 7) and the square root of 64 (which is 8). So 5 times √2, brings it down to a digestible number.

(I simplify √50 to √25 x √2. Then 5 times √2.)

This process reveals hidden patterns in numbers, gives exact values without rounding, and lets us manipulate irrational numbers in algebraic equations with precision. The beauty in simplifying surds comes from making complex, infinite decimals manageable while retaining their accuracy and integrity.

Surds help us understand and work with irrational numbers. While irrational numbers cannot be represented as exact fractions or decimals, surds allow us to use them precisely without approximation.

Surds are essential in algebra and geometry, especially when working with Pythagorean theorem, trigonometry, and quadratic equations, which often result in square roots or other roots that are irrational.

Learning to simplify surds prepares students for higher maths topics, such as calculus and complex number theory, where understanding irrational values becomes essential.

In mathematics, exact answers are often preferable to rounded ones. Surds allow us to express values like $\sqrt{2}$ or $\sqrt{3}$ exactly, which can be crucial in theoretical work or when calculating precise measurements.

Real-life uses

Engineering and construction: Surds are used in engineering for precise calculations, especially when dealing with measurements and angles that involve square roots. For example, the diagonal of a square is expressed as a surd (e.g., side length $\sqrt{2}$), which is used in designing and constructing buildings.

Architecture and design: When calculating the dimensions for structural design, architects often encounter surds in measurements (like the hypotenuse in right-angled triangles). Using surds allows accurate scaling.

Physics and wave calculations: In physics, surds often appear in sound, when calculating wave frequencies, amplitudes, or other properties that involve roots of non-square numbers. Using surds helps physicists and engineers maintain precision.

Computer graphics and animation: Surds are used in rendering graphics, especially for transformations involving irrational numbers. For example, the scaling factor of $\sqrt{2}$ appears in certain symmetrical transformations.

Finance and economics: While less common, surds occasionally arise in compound interest formulas and in the study of financial algorithms where non-integer growth rates require precise calculations.

In essence, surds provide a practical way to work with irrational numbers without sacrificing accuracy, which has applications across fields where precision is critical. Their study teaches us to appreciate the exactness and patterns in numbers, highlighting the beauty of mathematics.

28th December 2024

48 Teaching VIII

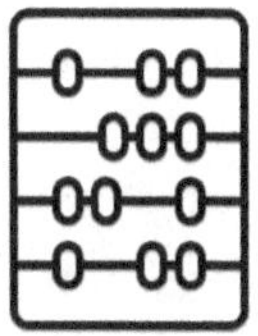

Subtracting fear, adding confidence: Maths in the classroom

'I hated Maths at school.' | 'I'm not good at Maths.' | 'I could never be a teacher.'

These are some common phrases that one hears, when you tell people that you're a Maths teacher.

At this, I remember the question that Sir John Drummond used to ask people who claimed that they didn't understand modern classical music: 'Are you boasting or apologising?' I ask the same thing. They are never sure which one it is.

There are a few ways to learn Maths, and to teach it. My favourite one is to just keep practicing.

The countries with the world's top Maths attainment are Singapore, China, Hong Kong, South Korea, Finland, Japan, and Estonia - as measured by the PISA league tables *(Programme for International Student Assessment).*

These nations have some influential philosophies and approaches in mathematics education that other countries, including the United Kingdom (which has improved its attainment in the last ten years), have tried to copy and emulate.

Maths Mastery

Main idea: Rooted in theories of cognitive science, Maths Mastery emphasises deep understanding over procedural fluency. The goal is for students to gain a strong foundational understanding before moving on, reducing reliance on memory. Concepts are broken down, with a focus on understanding why methods work.

In practice: Students learn through concrete examples, pictorial representations, and finally abstract reasoning. Concepts are revisited regularly to build retention and understanding, and problem-solving is integrated throughout. The UK's *National Centre for Excellence in the Teaching of Mathematics* (NCETM) supports this method, and many UK primary schools have adopted the approach.

Outcomes and results: Schools adopting Maths Mastery report improvements in student engagement and understanding. UK studies by the *Education Endowment Foundation* have shown moderate positive effects on mathematics achievement. Additionally, countries that inspired this approach, like Singapore and China, consistently outperform others in mathematics.

Direct instruction

Main Idea: Developed to maximise the teacher's role in learning, Direct Instruction is a structured, teacher-led approach that emphasises clear, explicit teaching with specific steps and examples. The philosophy rests on the belief that skills and knowledge should be transmitted directly to students with high levels of clarity and repetition. It has been championed by influential American educationalists, like E.D. Hirsch and Barak Rosenshine.

In practice: Teachers break down complex concepts into smaller, teachable parts. Rosenshine's *Principles of Instruction* is a classic, short guide that walks teachers through steps that include checking previous learning, modelling, guided practice, and independent practice. Regular questioning, feedback loops and *Checking for Understanding* ensure that students are absorbing the content before moving on. This is known as *formative assessment,* to quickly check what students know, in real time. *Summative assessment,* in contrast, means tests and exams, which can periodically give a more official progress score.

Outcomes and results: Numerous studies demonstrate that Direct Instruction improves test scores, especially in students who struggle with traditional methods. A 2006 study from the *American Institutes for Research* found that Direct Instruction raised mathematics scores significantly in early education. By focusing on high-clarity lessons and structured practice, this approach can effectively reduce achievement gaps.

Doug Lemov's Teach Like a Champion

Doug Lemov is a teacher and school principal. He helped found *Uncommon Schools,* a network of high performing schools in under-served communities. His best-selling book *Teach Like a Champion,* is revolutionising classrooms around the world.

Main idea: Lemov's approach emphasises classroom management, teacher clarity, and behaviour strategies, advocating for high engagement and academic rigour. While it covers all subject areas, it has valuable insights for maths instruction, especially on fostering an environment that promotes learning.

In practice: Techniques like 'Cold Call' (asking any student a question without prior warning) and 'No Opt Out' (ensuring students answer every question) create an accountable and inclusive atmosphere. Lemov emphasises the use of 'Ratio' (getting students to do more of the thinking and talking in class) and 'Checking for Understanding' to ensure all students are following the lesson.

Outcomes and results: Schools using *Teach Like a Champion* techniques, such as Success Academies in New York, and the Michaela School in London, have demonstrated high achievement, particularly with historically underperforming demographics. The focus on engagement and rigour creates disciplined, focused classrooms that facilitate deep learning and strong maths performance.

Inquiry-based approaches

This seems to be the trendy method of the moment. To me, it's the one that seems most useless and tiresome.

Main idea: Students construct their own understanding through exploration and problem-solving, rather than passively receiving knowledge. Inquiry-based learning encourages students to ask questions, investigate, and discover answers through exploration.

In practice: Teachers act as facilitators, guiding students as they work through real-life problems or projects. Students often work collaboratively, and lessons are more discussion-driven than lecture-based. This approach aims to develop critical thinking and self-directed learning.

Outcomes and results: Research shows that while inquiry-based approaches develop problem-solving skills and engagement, they can lead to inconsistent outcomes in standardised test performance. A 2016 *PISA* report noted that while such methods foster enjoyment and engagement, they are most effective when paired with structured instruction.

These techniques only really work *after* you have used direct instruction, and they more often find fertile ground with more able, higher-prior attaining students. With less able students, you often get rabbits trapped in headlights.

Socratic discussion

Main idea: The Socratic method uses questioning and dialogue to help students arrive at mathematical conclusions through reasoning. It is particularly common in advanced maths education, promoting deep understanding and critical thinking.

In practice: Teachers ask open-ended questions and challenge students to defend their answers. Classes become collaborative, with students encouraged to question each other and to discuss different strategies for solving problems.

Outcomes and results: This approach promotes high engagement and critical thinking but can be challenging in large or under-resourced classrooms. Studies have shown that it is beneficial for developing analytical skills and confidence, though it's often paired with more structured methods for balanced outcomes.

Summary

Evidence suggests that a balanced approach, blending explicit instruction with opportunities for inquiry and problem-solving, tends to yield the best results. The most effective strategies often depending on the students' age, prior knowledge, and the context of the classroom.

3rd January 2025

49 One

1

The Power of One

Read a few pages of a newspaper or a magazine. Write down every number that you see. An incredible pattern will emerge. It happens everywhere - in stock market prices, the census data of populations, and river lengths.

It's called *Benford's law*. The rule states that 30 per cent of the numbers you see will start with a 1. And 18 per cent of them will start with a 2, and right down to 4.6 per cent of the numbers starting with 9.

It's a law so unexpected that many people simply refuse to believe that it can be true. But it is.

If all digits were represented equally, then they would each appear one ninth (about 11.1 per cent) of the time. The law holds even when you change the units of your data. Measure rivers in feet or metres, measure stock prices in dollars or sterling – any way you measure, these exact proportions of leading digits remain.

Discovery

Before calculators, people solved tough arithmetic using reference books called logarithm tables. In 1881 astronomer

Simon Newcomb noticed that the early pages of logarithm tables, which correspond to numbers beginning with 1, were much more grubby and worn out than the later pages. He deduced that smaller leading digits must be more common in natural data sets, and he published the correct percentages.

Physicist Frank Benford made the same observation in 1938 and popularised the law, compiling more than 20,000 data points to demonstrate its universality.

To illustrate why the rule works, imagine an island that is inhabited by 100 animals, and whose population doubles every year. After one year there are 200 animals, and after two years there are 400. For the first year, the first digit of the population of the island was a 1. In the second year population count spanned the 200s and 300s in the same length of time, leaving less time for each leading digit to apply. This continues with 400 to 800 in the third year, when the leading digits retire even faster.

Growing from 1,000 to 2,000 requires doubling (a 100% increase), whereas growing from 8,000 to 9,000 is only a 12.5% increase.

Application

The law has been used to put people behind bars. Financial adviser Wesley Rhodes was convicted of defrauding investors when prosecutors argued in court that his documents did not follow the expected distribution of leading digits and therefore were fraudulent.

The principle helped computer scientist Jennifer Golbeck uncover a Russian bot network on *Twitter*. She observed that for most users, the number of followers that their followers have adheres to Benford's law, but artificial accounts significantly veer from this pattern.

Benford's law is often applied to fraud detection: from Greece manipulating macroeconomic data when applying to join the Euro, to vote rigging in Iran's 2009 presidential election. The message is clear: organic processes generate numbers that favour small leading digits, whereas falsified data does not.

Deviations from Benford's law might indicate errors or fraudulent activities. In digital image forensics, for example, analysing the distribution of leading digits in image files helps to identify any manipulated or suspect images.

It's worth stating that some data sets don't conform to Benford's law. Adult heights mostly begin with 4, 5 and 6 when measured in feet. A roulette wheel is equally likely to land on a number beginning with 2 as on a number beginning with 1.

While Benford's law is a useful tool, it's not fool-proof, but it can raise a flag and prompt further investigation.

28th March 2024

X – Books

'Philosophy: noun,

A route of many roads, leading from nowhere to nothing.'

— Ambrose Bierce, *The Devil's Dictionary*

50 85

The 85 ways to tie a tie

Evidence of the earliest known knotted neckcloth lies in the tomb of China's first emperor, Qin Shih-huang-di (259 - 210 BCE). In an elaborate underground mausoleum, 7,500 sculptured terracotta soldiers each sport knotted neckerchiefs.

Two Cambridge University mathematicians, Thomas Fink and Yong Mao, have researched the physics and equations of tying a necktie. Their research paper was published in the respected science journals *Nature* and *Physica A*.

The authors prove that there are exactly 85 ways of tying a necktie using the conventional method of wrapping the wide end of the tie around the narrow end. They describe each one, and highlight those that they determine to be historically notable or aesthetically pleasing.

The mathematics

The discovery of all possible ways to tie a tie depends on a mathematical formulation of knots being equivalent to *persistent random walks* on a *triangular lattice,* with some constraints on how the walks begin and end. Thus enumerating tie knots of n moves is equivalent to enumerating walks of n steps.

The basic idea is that tie knots can be described as a sequence of five different possible moves: left (L), centre (C), right (R), into (i), out (o), and through the loop (T). With this shorthand, traditional and new knots can be compactly expressed. Any knot that begins with an **o** move must start with the tie turned inside out around the neck.

The authors turned their academic paper into a popular book which is a delight to read. Fink and Mao provide an informative history of tie-knot evolution. They also provide much more – a guide to taste in knot tying. The book shows which knot works best with a given tie and collar, and shows that tie knots that can be enjoyed as things of beauty in themselves.

Fink and Mao have performed a great service for civilisation, doing for tie-knot tying what Isaac Newton did for the motion of the heavens: lifting it from the darkness of secrecy, ritual and superstition to the light of rational, scientific good taste. The scientific force of the work is that Fink and Mao have created a formal model that captures the salient characteristics of tie-knot tying in the real world, and have then analysed the formal model, guided by the scientific lights of simplicity and symmetry. Their model predicts the knots most commonly used, and provides several new possibilities.

Fink and Mao have obeyed the imperative of the scientific entrepreneur: create a niche, and then fill it. Their book is the definitive work on tie knots, and on one of the most common applications of knot theory.

The applications of knot theory are infinite: a test tube of DNA may contain billions of knots, but sometimes they are hard to see. Polymers in general may gain many of their characteristics from tangling, knotting and linking, but this may not be apparent when you are holding the material in your hand. Magnetic field lines are often knotted, linked or otherwise entangled. But now imagine the morning dressing routines around the world – imagine how many tie knots are tied in a day.

Fink and Mao have shown that it is possible to be both smart and smart – in brains and in style. Symmetry in tie knots refers to two qualities: visual symmetry (the knot appears to be shaped identically on the left and right), and mathematical symmetry (the number of L and R moves being as close to equal as possible).

21st December 2023

51 Bloom

Bloom and Potter

Harold Bloom was the Sterling Professor of Humanities at *Yale University*, from 1983 to 2019. He wrote over fifty books - most notable being, *The Anxiety of Influence (1973), The Western Canon* (1994), and *Shakespeare: The Invention of the Human* (1998).

The most formidable scholar, teacher and critic of his generation, he combined deep learning - trained in the rabbinical tradition of Torah study - with an uncompromising defence of the Western literary tradition. His detractors charged him with elitism. He countered with 3,000 years of evidence, from Homer to Hemingway. He spoke only Yiddish and read only Hebrew up until the age of six.

When asked about the Old and New Testaments, he answered, 'I prefer to call them the Original Testament and the Belated Testament.'

Interviewer: *How would you suggest interesting a young person in today's society in the benefits of reading?*

Bloom: I compiled an anthology, out of my negative reaction of the prevalence of the Harry Potter books, which seem to me, rubbish. Only good for the dustbin, where they will certainly wind up, in a generation or so.

The anthology, '*Stories and Poems for Extremely Intelligent Children of All Ages*', was meant as an introduction to a great many appropriate pieces.

Interviewer: *If you have a young person who doesn't like to read?*

Bloom: It's an interesting puzzle. A lot of people have people have said to me that it's all very well for me to deplore the Harry Potter books, but nevertheless this is the one thing that their children will read. I think the real question is what will they read after they have read Harry Potter? Will they go on to *Alice in Wonderland,* and then *Through the Looking Glass*? Will they go on to Kenneth Graham's *The Wind in the Willows*? Will they go on to high literature? Will they go on to Mark Twain, and to Hemingway, and eventually Jane Austen?

I thought in a way, that the novelist Stephen King - whose work does not move me - got this quite right. I don't think he was being ironic. In his *Sunday Times* book review of the fourth volume in the Potter series, he welcomed it, and said this is wonderful. He said if they are reading this when they are ten or eleven or twelve, then they will graduate to reading Stephen King a year or two later. I would not argue with him, at all, about that.

We cannot be happy about the millions of copies sold of Harry Potter. That's not reading. They're just an endless string of cliches.

Interviewer: *But then what are you saying, that millions of people are wrong?*

Bloom: I'm afraid so. It's fashion. The current thing.

Solitary reading is an endowment. It will survive everything. Readers will find something deep within themselves.

Possession by memory - you cannot overestimate the power of memory. Without memory you can't think, or do anything. You have to train the memory. The only way to do it is by yourself.

The cultural critics will introduce Harry Potter into their college curriculum, and *The New York Times* will celebrate the dumbing-down it exemplifies.

Teaching can help. But there has to be an initial vocation, or gift. An impulse towards deep reading.

My students today are the children of students I once taught at Yale. In their time, their parents read more because there were fewer distractions. Today's students are wonderful readers. They just need to be left alone, and told, there is nothing better for you to be doing than solitary reading.

I owe everything to the *Bronx Public Library.*

12th September 2024

52 Dracula

Grim tales from rural Transylvania

'The children of the night. Such music they make.'
— Bela Lugosi, Dracula (1931)

Vampire origins

The myths and legends about vampires have ancient roots that can be traced back thousands of years.

Some of the earliest vampire-like creatures appear in ancient Mesopotamian mythology, around 4,000 years ago. The Akkadian myth mentions Lilitu, a female demon associated with the night who was believed to prey on men and children.

The ancient Greeks and Romans had their own vampiric figures, such as the Lamia, a female demon who drank the blood of young men, and the Empusa, a shape-shifting demon who also fed on blood.

The most direct predecessors to the modern vampire myth come from Slavic and Eastern European folklore. Stories of vampires (known as 'vampir' in Serbian, 'upyr' in Russian) began to emerge in these regions around the medieval era, during the 11th and 12th centuries.

These vampires were known as 'the undead' – corpses that had risen from their graves to drink the blood of the living. They were typically associated with disease, death, and evil spirits. Rituals to prevent the dead from becoming vampires included burying them with a stake in their heart, decapitation, or placing garlic in their mouth.

During the 17th and 18th centuries, vampire panic spread across parts of Western Europe, especially in Austria and Hungary. This was fuelled by the spread of folklore as people moved westward. These tales contributed to the European belief in vampires as malevolent creatures.

Bram Stoker's 'Dracula' and inspirations

Irish writer Abraham Stoker's 1897 novel '*Dracula*' is the most famous vampire story in Western literature, and it drew inspiration from a variety of sources.

Stoker was inspired by the vampire myths of Eastern Europe, particularly those from Transylvania, Romania. He incorporated many traditional vampire traits from this folklore, such as the need to drink blood, the ability to shape-shift, and an aversion to crucifixes and sunlight.

Stoker drew inspiration from Vlad III Dracula, also known as Vlad the Impaler, a 15th-century ruler of Wallachia (modern-day Romania). Vlad was notorious for his brutal methods of punishing his enemies, including impalement, and his moniker 'Dracula' (meaning 'son of the dragon' or 'son of the devil') became associated with the vampire count in Stoker's novel.

Another fable of the time was the legend of Elizabeth Báthory, a Hungarian countess accused of murdering young women and bathing in their blood.

'The Vampyre' by John Polidori (1819) is often considered the first English vampire story. Polidori's vampire, Lord Ruthven, is a suave, aristocratic figure, which influenced the depiction of vampires as sophisticated and seductive.

Stoker was influenced by Mary Shelley's 'Frankenstein' and Edgar Allan Poe's stories, emphasising dark, mysterious, and supernatural elements.

Stoker reflected the social and cultural anxieties of his time, including fears of the unknown, the threat of foreign invaders, and concerns about sexual morality.

Hungarian actor Bela Lugosi's 1931 portrayal of the Count remains one of the most vividly memorable screen performances of any genre, creating the template for sinister sophistication that is widely imitated. *Sesame Street's* counting Count is pure Lugosi.

It gets weirder

The erotic implications of vampires have been the subject of some research, especially within women's fantasies.

The engineers at *Google,* on what must have been a very slow Friday afternoon, decided to analyse male and female web searches. Within the female data they segregated the typical female erotic preferences when searching for pornography. They found that women tend to prefer written, literary porn.

The main erotic fantasies that women have tend to adhere to one of these five main archetypes: *vampire, werewolf, billionaire, pirate* and *surgeon*.

19th August 2024

❧❧❧

53 Brighton

Echo

'This is the coastal town, that they forgot to close down.'
— Morrissey, *Everyday is Like Sunday*

This summer (2024), I read *Brighton Rock* by Graham Greene for the first time. It was immensely enjoyable. An immersive novel that takes you into a 1930s world of petty criminals – the racetrack, the chip-shop, the tea room, the noisy pub with its *end-of-the-pier* entertainments. The seaside town as a metaphor for escape (from London) and hibernation (from those after you).

The gang of characters – Dallow, Spicer, Pinkie and Cubitt – cut a Dickensian swagger.

But really, I was much more sorry to say goodbye to Rose and Ida. Rose is seventeen, innocent, and easily led; Ida is the world-weary, instinctive crusader.

I missed them when I finished the novel. So, here is my storyboard outline: for a sequel.

Title: The Echo of Brighton

Part One: Aftermath

Rose is left reeling from the bleak realisation that Pinkie, the man she loved, despised her.

Rose returns to the squalid rooms she once shared with Pinkie, but Brighton has become a place filled with many painful memories. She decides to leave, taking up work as a chambermaid in a nearby coastal town, to distance herself from her past.

Part Two: A new start

In her new town, Rose meets Margaret, an older, no-nonsense widow who runs the boarding house where Rose finds a room. Margaret becomes a surrogate mother to Rose, providing her with guidance and stability, and encourages her to look forward. Margaret introduces Rose to her nephew Jack, a dockworker with a rough charm, who is drawn to Rose's vulnerability.

Despite Jack's interest, Rose remains emotionally distant, haunted by her memories. However, through Jack's persistence and genuine affection they start a relationship, with Jack offering Rose the normal life she never thought possible.

Part Three: Confronting the past

Ida Arnold reappears in Rose's life, visiting her unexpectedly. Ida is moved to see Rose still struggling with her past. She urges Rose to confront the reality of what Pinkie was – a monster who manipulated and abused her.

At the same time, Rose encounters Father McCarthy, a kindly priest who serves the local parish. Rose confides in him, wrestling with her belief that she is damned because of her association with Pinkie. Father McCarthy helps Rose to seek forgiveness and redemption.

Part Four: A flicker of hope

Jack proposes, but Rose hesitates, torn between the possibility of happiness and her belief that she does not deserve it.

Meanwhile, Rose begins volunteering at a local charity, helping destitute women and children. This work gives her purpose and rebuilds her self-esteem.

Part Five: Final choice

As Rose slowly heals, she is faced with a final test. A mobster from Brighton tracks her down. He offers her a large sum of money to remain silent about what she knows of the gang's activities, hinting at the dangers that still lurk if she doesn't comply. This encounter shakes Rose, reminding her that she is not yet free from her past.

Rose turns to Father McCarthy, who counsels her to reject the offer and to continue living honestly, even if it means exposing herself to danger. Rose, finally seeing the futility of trying to escape her past, decides to confront it head-on. She refuses the money and, with Jack's support, agrees to testify against the gang if called upon to do so, in a forthcoming trial.

Part Six: Echo

Rose marries Jack in a modest ceremony. She is determined to build a new life based on love, honesty, and service to others. Rose can choose to live differently. The echoes of Brighton remain, but they now no longer define her.

12th October 2024

XI – Places

'At every party there are two kinds of people – those who want to go home and those who don't.
The trouble is, they are usually married to each other.'

— Ann Landers, *The New Yorker*

54 Corridors

Green pathways

How Medellin is beating the heat

Oriental Avenue, a street in Medellín, Colombia, is covered with large fruit trees, shrubs and flowers. Residents say that both the local air quality and temperature have improved.

Medellín, Colombia's second largest city after Bogotá, started its 'green corridors' programme in 2016 due to concern about air pollution and rising heat.

Composed of more than 30 green corridors, it connects newly-greened road verges, vertical gardens, streams, parks and nearby hills. The project involved planting 120,000 individual plants and 12,500 trees on roads and in parks, with 2.5 million new smaller plants and 880,000 trees planted across the city.

The idea was to connect green spaces in the city together through avenues and streets surrounded by trees and shade. Vegetation absorbs air pollutants and improves air quality, while also sucking up planet-heating carbon emissions.

Concentrations of concrete and black tarmac roads in such areas absorb the sun's heat and then radiate it back out, keeping cities hotter even after sunset, according to the United Nations Environment Programme (UNEP).

The initial investment to establish the project cost a total of $16.3m (£13.2m) and an annual maintenance cost of $625,000 (£504,000) in 2022.

Medellín's approach to green corridors offers a low-cost, popular solution which other cities are increasingly looking to replicate.

Could it be a model for a climate-resilient city of the future?

Alongside worries about urban heat, Medellín's green corridors project addressed concerns of poor air quality, caused by growth in private transport.

A 2020 study from the University of Antioquia in Medellín concluded that 1,971 premature deaths were caused by pollution in the Aburrá Valley in 2016. It warned that deaths from pollution would increase substantially by 2030 in the absence of controls on emissions from vehicles. The corridors act as 'green barriers' against dangerous particulate matter, absorbing a significant amount of pollution.

Alongside the 30 green corridors, 124 parks are also part of the project, connected by the corridors and planted with new vegetation. This rise in greenery across the city is also having a positive climate impact. A 2019 study from the University of Engineering of Antioquia estimated that just two of these parks, the Nutibara and Volador Hills, were responsible for removing 40 tonnes of carbon dioxide (CO2) per year from the atmosphere.

Local people choose initiatives they want to be funded

The local community has chosen many green initiatives for the city, and maintain the scheme by volunteering as gardeners. The green corridors project hires people arriving in Medellín displaced by violence in Colombia, helping them find permanent jobs.

Monitoring of local wildlife has seen birds, lizards, frogs and bats in the corridor, which had not been seen in the city for years. This has helped to keep rats and other pests under control.

These achievements have made the project famous, and other cities such as Bogotá and Barranquilla have adopted similar plans. South America's biggest city, São Paulo in Brazil, expanded its version of the corridors.

'Public space can't be grey and full of cement. You have to change the concept of public space. We have to live together with nature,' said Natalia Urrego, Medellin's infrastructure secretary.

Maintaining the city's green corridors costs $1.50 per square metre every two months, based on work done by 150 gardeners. City Hall is looking for partnerships with private investors and businesses to sponsor a corridor.

Putting this idea into practice requires a shift in investment priorities, with city leaders spending too little on climate-friendly solutions despite pledges to promote a green COVID-19 recovery.

7th February 2024

55 Cult

Fear and loathing among the under-30s

'Traditions are experiments that worked.'
— Louise Perry

Orwell said that England is 'the only great country whose intellectuals are ashamed of their own nationality'. He wrote that 82 years ago, and nothing has changed.

The war on the West is also a civil war. It's a difficult one to understand.

The tradition – that gave us healthcare, stable governance, education, the rule of law, tolerance, freedom of expression, human rights, robust institutions, trustworthy courts, trade, and democracy – is being attacked from those who have benefited most from it.

In our staffroom recently, I jovially complained that the school had got rid of paper cups for coffee, and that we had to bring our own mugs.

It's all pointless, I said, as most of the pollution in the oceans comes from Vietnam, The Philippines, Indonesia,

China and India. The UK is responsible for an infinitesimally tiny proportion.

I was immediately challenged with comments from two twenty-something teachers. Things like, 'They make products for us', 'It's for our greed'.

'But it's mainly discarded fishing nets,' I vainly persisted. Their lightning quick response was, 'They're fishing for us'.

Whilst we do import a proportion of our fish from Asia, it's quite a leap to blame us for aquatic litter 10,000 km away. We get most of our fish from Scotland, Norway, and the EU.

Their automatic reaction was that we in the West are wrong. It's our fault. How dare you challenge people from the emerging, developing nations and apportion any blame on them. They're serving us; we should change our habits.

The teachers in the staffroom are educated people. Perhaps they were winding me up.

These teachers are friends, and they're likeable, decent people. We socialise, and we play football after school on Fridays. But I fear that they're in the grip of a cult that wouldn't have someone like me as a member.

Optimism

To end on a positive note. There is hope.

When Lord Coe was leading Britain's bid to host the 2012 Olympic Games, he was at an *International Olympic Committee* function in Japan. He was regaling the challenges, complexities and headaches of the London Olympic bid to a local Japanese dignitary. There was an insightful moment.

The local leader had been around a long time. He was cultivated, and smart. It was a year before the Games.

He looked at the worried Lord Coe and said, 'Why are you nervous?' He sighed. 'You are strange people in Britain. You are running large parts of the global economy, most of my colleagues and friends have been educated at some stage in Britain, our children want to be in Britain. If they don't want to be educated there, they want to start their careers there. If they don't want to do that, they want to come across to your theatres, your clubs. You do pageantry. You do Wimbledon. You do the Grand National. You do Cup Finals. What are you worried about?'

Coe realised that we have a 'monstrous ability in the UK to doubt our own ability'. And there was this guy, in Tokyo, into his early seventies, saying, 'This is going to be OK.'

24th March 2023

56 Kuwait

Yalla, الي (Arabic): let's go, hurry up, come on.

Speed

Between 2002 to 2004, I visited Kuwait many times.

While I was working at IBM, we had won a digital technology project with Kuwait's *Petrochemical Industries Company (PIC)*, to improve their business processes and to implement new systems for finance, supply chain, human resources and engineering. I was usually in the country for a couple of weeks at a time. And then home for a bit. The longest, single stretch of time that I was in Kuwait for, was five weeks.

On arrival, I met some Brits, who took me under their wing. One such was Tony Turner, who worked for a company called *eSolutions*. He had been in the region for years, and was experienced in projects similar to my own. Tony gave me two excellent pieces of advice - I still use them today.

Kuwait probably has the worst drivers in the world. They drive fast and recklessly. So, when driving in Kuwait, Tony said, imagine that you have large bouncy tyres around your car, and make sure you always keep several car distances away from any other car that you see. If a car is coming up to overtake you, slow down and let it pass you quickly. If you are about to overtake a car, do it swiftly, and get out of their range. Basically, maintain a *safe zone* around you, and be well clear of any moving object.

Secondly, Tony said, if you are near another car, imagine the *most stupid thing* that that driver could do: then prepare for *that thing*.

Over the next two years, I lost count of the number of *Porsche's* or *Cadillac's* on their roof, blocking a lane of the highway. Thankfully, I was never in an accident, largely due to Tony's advice.

'Work'

A co-worker from Pakistan memorably quipped: 'Why are these Kuwaitis always rushing? When they get to their destination, they have nothing to do!'

Kuwait has four million inhabitants. A million are Kuwaiti nationals, and three million are foreign workers. It is these foreign workers who actually get things done in the country. These immigrant workers are from the USA, the UK, India, Pakistan, Bangladesh, Egypt, the Philippines, the Lebanon. Some of the Indian and Pakistani professionals that I met - engineers, accountants, project managers, computer specialists - had not been home for a few years. They sent money home, but rarely travelled back.

Kuwaiti nationals are treated very well by their government. They almost all have government jobs - in the oil and gas industry, telecommunications, banking, and local government. Managerial positions and director level jobs. Jobs for life. Most young Kuwaitis I worked with had studied at US or UK universities. When a Kuwaiti gets married to a Kuwaiti woman, he get $100,000 from the government. He gets nothing if he marries a non-Kuwaiti woman.

Kuwaitis pray five times a day. Tea-boys at the offices constantly make coffee and tea. Very little work gets done. However, the Kuwaitis are a hospitable people, and whilst highly traditional, they do seek a modern outlook in matters of science and engineering.

Fearless

I was in Kuwait either side of the second Iraq War (2003). Before the war, our hotel - *The Hilton Kuwait Resort* - had several rooms occupied by American companies *KBR* and *Halliburton*, on lucrative Pentagon contracts. Their logos sellotaped to the doors. They provided logistics services, in anticipation of oncoming military operations.

Halliburton was the US military's biggest contractor in Iraq, with contracts worth $8 billion, for delivering mail, cooking meals, providing facilities maintenance management, sanitation services, building bases and repairing Iraq's oil industry.

A tip for you: whenever you see American corporations shipping in medical supplies and vacuum-packed, freeze-dried food - that's a sure-fire sign: *war is a-comin'*.

17th August 2023

57 Kuwait II

The time value of money

Cost

In 2004, I worked in Kuwait for around 8 months. I travelled in and out on a monthly basis.

The work was to implement new business processes and enterprise wide technology systems - *Oracle, Maximo* and *AspenTech* - for our client, the Kuwait *Petrochemicals Industries Company* (*PIC*). *PIC* manufactured industrial fertilisers, Ammonia and Urea, for export to global markets.

One of our team, a Canadian consultant, was leading a workstream called *Activity-Based Costing*. This was a method of capturing and reporting costs at each stage of a process. The client's leadership could then see which steps were too costly, and then simplify or eliminate them, to reduce costs.

Our Canadian consultant was having trouble convincing the client team on the ground to be engaged and interested in this workstream. He explained the value of capturing costs at a detailed level, and the insights it could bring.

His client project team wouldn't play, and he was getting frustrated.

He was telling me his troubles in our hotel's *Starbucks* one Saturday morning.

After our cappuccinos and blueberry muffins, we got into our hire car – a small *Hyundai* saloon – and headed to the central shopping centre. There wasn't much else to do in Kuwait in 2004. Restaurants, cafes, malls.

On our way to the mall, we stopped at a petrol station to refuel the car. This being Kuwait, with its abundant oil and gas reserves, you could fill a car with petrol for about the same price as a cappuccino and a blueberry muffin.

As the gas station attendant was refuelling our car, I asked him (an Indian, obviously), for a full car wash once he'd finished at the petrol pump.

He then drove the car round to the car wash area. Out of nowhere, around a dozen Indian workers in flip-flops and blue overalls appeared and got to work washing, rinsing and polishing the car, inside and out.

It was a manual process – a highly labour-intensive effort.

Then it hit us. My Canadian colleague was commenting on how many people it took to wash the car. Twelve. He was amazed at the sheer quantity of foreign labour.

I said to him, 'So, now you know why your client guys don't give a damn about *Activity-Based Costing*. How much does it cost to employ this mini army of Indian workmen, all working super-fast to clean our car?'

'Probably peanuts', he replied.

'Exactly,' I said. 'Labour is so cheap – especially from South-East Asia.'

The Kuwaitis couldn't be bothered with counting the cost of these *activities*. It was a rounding error. What they were really interested in was the cost of the spare parts to keep the critical equipment working in the factory. I asked the Canadian, 'How much does a compressor or a turbine or a valve or a pump from *General Electric* or *Rolls-Royce* or *Siemens* cost?'

'A compressor? That's about two million dollars!'

'Yep. So that's the cost they're focused on. They want to maintain and inspect that critical part, so that it works reliably and predictably. So that it lasts, and won't fail. That's what interests them.'

The mist cleared. Someone somewhere might be interested in how much the Human Resource department (Indians, of course) spent on recruitment and screening CVs from new applicants for open jobs. Or how much the Finance department spent on closing the books at each month-end. But, it was like moving deckchairs on the Titanic. It wasn't going to move the needle on the corporate dashboard.

Pareto was right. 80:20. Focus on the 20% of activities that account for 80% of the true value. You just know that the remaining 80% of the activities are just noise.

28th September 2023

58 Kuwait III

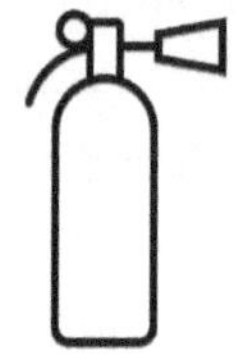

'And the fifth angel sounded, and I saw a star fall from heaven unto the earth. And there arose a smoke of a great furnace; and the sun and the air were darkened by reason of the smoke.'

— Werner Herzog, quoting Revelation 9: 1-2 in his film *Lessons of Darkness*

Iraq invaded its neighbour Kuwait on 2nd August 1990. In two days, the Iraqis established Kuwait as one of its regions and occupied the country for seven months.

The UN Security Council authorised an international coalition to expel Iraqi troops from Kuwait, and initiated the First Gulf War on 17th January 1991.

As the war effort continued over the next month, Iraq fired missiles at Israel. The Iraqi government had hoped that an Israeli retaliation would prompt the coalition's Muslim-majority states to rescind their support for the campaign against Iraq. However, no such retaliation took place, and the coalition began a ground invasion of Iraqi-occupied Kuwait and parts of Iraq on 23rd February 1991.

As Iraqi troops retreated from Kuwait, they set fire to over 700 Kuwaiti oil wells, but this was unsuccessful in thwarting the coalition. By 28th February 1991, the Iraqi military had been devastated and Kuwaiti independence was restored.

Kuwaiti oil fires

The oil well fires were started in January and February 1991, and the first fires were extinguished in early April 1991, with the last well capped in November, 1991.

Smoke plumes could be seen from the *Space Shuttle Atlantis* during its orbital flights.

Concerted efforts to bring the fires under control began in April 1991. The accumulated financial losses were estimated to be $160 billion USD, representing 10% of Kuwait's 90 billion barrels of oil reserves, according to *KOC*, the *Kuwait Oil Company*.

Extinguishing efforts

It was predicted by experts that, if left alone, the fires would burn for between two and five years, before losing pressure and going out on their own.

The companies responsible for extinguishing the fires were *Bechtel, Red Adair Company, Boots & Coots International Well Control, Wild Well Control* and *Safety Boss*.

According to Larry Flak, a petroleum engineer for *Boots & Coots*, 90% of all the fires were put out by sea water, sprayed from powerful hoses at the base of the fire. The extinguishing water was supplied to the desert region by re-purposing the oil pipelines that had previously pumped oil from the wells to the Arabian Gulf.

For the more stubborn oil fires, the use of a gas turbine to blast a large volume of water at high velocity at the fire proved popular with firefighters, and was brought to the region by Hungarian engineers equipped with engines from *MiG-21* fighter planes. The engines were mounted onto battlefield T-34 tanks. This technique extinguished 9 fires in 43 days.

Another method used was to deploy high explosives, such as dynamite, to create a blast wave that pushed the burning fuel and local atmospheric oxygen away from the well. (This is exactly what happens when we blow out a candle.) The flame is removed and the fuel continues to spill out without igniting.

Explosives were placed inside 55 gallon drums surrounded by fire resistant chemicals, and then the drums are wrapped with insulating material with a horizontal crane being used to bring the drum as close to the burning area as possible.

Vegetation in most of the contaminated areas adjoining the oil lakes began recovering by 1995, but the dry climate also partially solidified some of the lakes. Over time the oil has continued to sink into the sand, with harmful consequences for Kuwait's small groundwater resources.

27th June 2024

59 Thames

Recently, I went for lunch with an ex-IBM work colleague and good friend, Jon Coles. We meet around twice a year. Rendezvous point was *The Albany* pub, on the banks of the river Thames, in a village called Thames Ditton, near Hampton Court.

On my walk there from Thames Ditton station, I passed the church of St Nicholas. A sign said, *'Church is Open. Please Come in.'* I did so. An ancient church. Cosy. Medieval. I donated £5 and looked around.

I saw a framed sign, written in italic fountain pen calligraphy, that just stopped me in my tracks.

It said, 'Vicars of Thames Ditton'. And listed the names of the clergymen who had served as parish priests here, and their years of office.

What gave me goosebumps, was that the list started from the year ... 1179.

Eleven seventy nine.

That's eight hundred and forty five (845) years ago.

Motionless, I read every year and every name. Almost a millennium of English history.

There were some gaps - unknown names, unknown dates. But they were continuous after 1649.

It takes a village

It got me thinking about life in 1179.

A picturesque glimpse into medieval life. The village is part of a larger feudal landscape, organised around agricultural rhythms and nature.

The village is a cluster of simple, thatched cottages made from wattle and daub, surrounded by fields and woodland. Homes are modest - a single room for living and sleeping. A loft for storage. Smoke from hearth fires rises from each roof, giving the air a smoky, earthy scent.

Daily Activities

Life revolves around agriculture and the river. The villagers are mostly serfs and free peasants who work the land owned by a local lord. They grow crops such as wheat, barley, and rye, and tend to vegetable gardens. Livestock like pigs, sheep, and chickens are common, providing meat, wool, and eggs.

Fishing is a significant part of life due to the village's proximity to the Thames. The river not only supplies fish, essential in the medieval diet, but also serves as a means of transport and communication. Small boats are common, carrying goods and people to and from the village.

Trade and Professions

Thames Ditton's economy is primarily subsistence-based, but some trade occurs, particularly with nearby villages and towns, such as Richmond, Hampton Wick, and Kingston. The river provides a route for trading surplus grain, fish, and wool. In exchange, the villagers acquire goods they cannot produce themselves, such as salt, leather, textiles, or pottery.

Professions in the village are few but essential. The blacksmith's forge is a key establishment, which produces tools, farming equipment, horseshoes, and weapons.

A miller operates a water mill on a tributary or a windmill on a hill, grinding grain into flour. The local alewife brews beer, a staple of the medieval diet, consumed by all ages as it's safer to drink than water.

Social and Cultural Life

The community is close-knit. Festivals and holy days are significant events, providing respite from the labour-intensive life. The villagers gather at harvest time, Christmas, Easter, and the Feast Day of St Nicholas, sharing food, stories, and entertainments.

The parish priest plays a central role in education and local governance. He teaches the village children basic reading and writing, using Latin, the language of the Church. The priest records significant events, such as births, marriages, deaths, and he may arbitrate in local disputes, maintaining the earliest semblance of local history.

Life is hard work, but with deep communal ties, and governed by the cycles of nature and the Church. A rhythm that's demanding and spiritually enriching.

5th September 2024

60 Israel

'We Jews have a secret weapon. We have no place to go.'

– Golda Meir, Fourth Prime Minister of Israel

Blood libel was the phrase given to an ancient lie, an antisemitic falsehood, that Jews killed Christian children to use their blood for religious ritual.

Modern versions exist. There are four blood libels used today by antisemites, that are just as widely believed, and just as false.

First, the libel of colonialism

Israel is the ultimate decolonisation success story. Against all odds, after Arab imperialism, Islamic conquest, and British colonialism, the Jews, indigenous to Judaea, re-established Israel. Yasser Arafat, who was born in Cairo, created Palestinian national identity in the 1960s, decades after the Palestinians were living in Jerusalem under Ottoman and then British rule. They had identity cards issued to them by the British, identifying them as Palestinians. Nationals of the 'British Mandate'.

Two, the libel of ethnic cleansing

In 1947, Israel was created as a nation. In 1948, five Arab armies attacked this fledgling state, with the stated intention of annihilating its people. 700,000 Arabs escaped the fighting. Those that remained became Israeli citizens. The Arab population of Israel has increased tenfold. This is not ethnic cleansing.

Ethnic cleansing is what happened to the Jews in 1948, when Jordan occupied the West Bank. And when 850,000 Jews were expelled from Yemen, Algeria, Egypt, Morocco, Syria, Lebanon and Iraq, where they had lived for thousands of years. Ethnic cleansing left Arab countries Jew free.

Meanwhile, two million Arabs live in Israel today.

Three, the libel of apartheid

Those Arabs that remained in Israel are now 20% of its population. They are among the most free Arabs in the Middle East. They are represented in every area of Israeli society: town Mayors, Army officers, Police commanders, members of Parliament, and Supreme Court judges. Arab political parties have formed part of governing coalitions. Arabic is one of the official languages of Israel.

Supreme Court judge Salim Joubran, an Arab, put both an Israeli Prime Minister and an Israeli President in jail. (Ehud Olmert and Moshe Katsav).

Those who propagate the lie of apartheid, seek to conflate Arab citizens of Israel, with Arabs living under the Palestinian Authority, who have autonomy and should be voting for their leadership. But President Mahmoud Abbas is in the 19th year of his 4 year term.

Four, the libel of genocide

A reprehensible smear - inverting reality. Hamas has spent 16 years embedding its terror infrastructure in mosques, schools, hospitals and ordinary homes. Its central military tactic is to use civilians as human shields.

In the face of these unprecedented challenges, the Israeli Defence Force has taken greater measures to prevent civilian casualties than any other army in history, far exceeding the requirements of international law.

This is not propaganda. This is verified and attested to on the ground by independent agencies, and documented extensively by military historian John Spencer, chair of Urban Warfare Studies, at the Modern War Institute. He concludes that Hamas wishes Palestinian civilians to be martyrs to their cause, and that Israel wishes to save them. Many modern military leaders frequently say that they would not be able to meet the standards set by Israel, in the precautions that it takes.

In 1947, there were 1.3 million Palestinians. Today, there are 14 million. This is the complete opposite of genocide.

If the Palestinians laid down all their weapons this afternoon, there would be a Palestinian state tomorrow morning.

If Israel laid down its weapons this afternoon, there would be no more Jews left tomorrow morning.

19th September 2024

61 Manhattan

August 2023: On holiday

Heathrow airport. An announcement.

'Ladies and gentlemen, United Airlines Flight 941 to Newark is now ready for boarding. We'd like to invite any serving or retired members of our Armed Forces to board first. And we thank you for your service.'

Just. Loved. That.

As well as conventional activities – *World Trade Center Memorial Museum, The Book of Mormon* on Broadway, and an evening at the *Greenwich Village Comedy Club* – I also ticked off two bucket list items: Running 5k in Central Park, and experiencing a Harlem Gospel choir church service.

Central Park 5k

A bright, beautiful, warm, New York morning. I joined the hundreds of regular morning joggers, and I ran 5k, avoiding the cyclists. New Yorkers say that jogging is cheaper than therapy, and much more effective.

Then I headed to Central Park South, for a celebratory *Starbucks* cappuccino.

While waiting for my order, a woman in her sixties (heavy coat, plastic bags) came in and declared loudly, '*This is MY property. You're all on MY property*.'

She looked at the array of drinks in the collection area, took the most colourful one - a pink, summery concoction - and promptly left her property.

Harlem

The next day, at the 9am mid-town meeting point for the *Harlem Sunday Morning Gospel Tour*, three large coaches each had a different sign stuck on their windscreens: 'Italian', 'English', 'French'.

I met Earl, our guide. He'd visited England, years ago, as an actor. He reminisced about Manchester and Stratford-On-Avon.

As we entered Harlem, we stopped at the *Apollo Theatre*, to pay homage to its amazing history of talent. Stevie Wonder, Billie Holiday, The Temptations, The Supremes, James Brown, The Jacksons, and Prince, all got their big breaks there. They each have their *Hall of Fame* stars embedded in the pavement outside. These artists all started in Gospel music, and were hugely influenced by it.

When The Beatles first landed at JFK airport, the first place they wanted to go to was the *Apollo*.

The coach then took us to a church for the Gospel choir service. It was musically impressive, with a strong community feeling. The pastor announced times for Bible study classes and choir practice.

He read out notices from the congregation.

'Dorothy would like everyone to know that she is recovering well from her surgery. And she thanks you all for your warm wishes.'

'Martha's daughter and grandchildren are visiting from out of town, so she'll be with them this weekend.'

Then on to the world famous *Cotton Club* for a buffet brunch. It was the 1920s nightspot of choice for movie stars, gangsters, and jazz lovers. (Today's *Cotton Club* is in a different location from the original, but kept the name.)

Earl mentioned Francis Coppola's eponymous film, listing the actors in it: 'Gregory Hines, Maurice Hines, Laurence Fishburne, Lonette McKee.'

I didn't recognise half these names. Then I realised. Earl was listing only the black actors in it. If it was me, I'd have said 'Richard Gere, Bob Hoskins, Diane Lane, and Nicolas Cage.' Point well made, Earl.

Honey

I arranged to meet a good family friend, Marianna Satanas, who's a Brit ex-pat New Yorker, and something of a technology *grande fromage* in the fashion world. Walking to meet her for dinner one evening, I passed two black women sitting outside with their young kids, on the lower steps of a brownstone house.

One of them called out after me, '*You look like the guy in Despicable Me*!'

I turned around laughing. '*Gru*', I shouted.

'*Oh! And you know his name too eh, honey?!*', she shot back with a cheeky grin.

26th September 2024

62 Shipping

Sirens of the tundra

The British maritime weather report is known as *The Shipping Forecast.* It is produced by the *Meteorological Office* and broadcast by BBC Radio 4 on behalf of the *Maritime and Coastguard Agency.*

The forecast dates back over 150 years. There are two broadcasts each day at 00:48 and 05:20. And a third one at weekends at 17:54.

The maritime regions around the United Kingdom have evocative and intriguing names: *Viking, North Utsire, South Utsire, Forties, Cromarty, Forth, Tyne, Dogger, Fisher, German Bight, Humber, Thames, Dover, Wight, Portland, Plymouth, Biscay, Trafalgar, FitzRoy, Sole, Lundy, Fastnet, Irish Sea, Shannon, Rockall, Malin, Hebrides, Bailey, Fair Isle, Faeroes,* and *Southeast Iceland.*

The forecast gives the wind direction and force, atmospheric pressure, visibility and the state of the sea, for each of these regions.

Dependable, reassuring and never hurried, it is a voice of calm across the airwaves.

Influence

The Shipping Forecast is immensely popular with the British public. It attracts listeners in the hundreds of thousands daily - far more than actually require it.

In 1995, a plan to move the late night broadcast by 12 minutes triggered angry newspaper editorials and debates in the UK Parliament, and was ultimately scrapped. Similar outcry greeted the Met Office's decision to rename *Finisterre* to *FitzRoy*, but in that case, the decision was carried through.

Peter Jefferson, who read the forecast for 40 years until 2009, received letters from listeners saying that the 00:48 broadcast helped them get to sleep after a long day.

The Controller of BBC Radio 4, Mark Damazer, explained its popularity: 'It scans poetically. It's got a rhythm of its own. It's eccentric, it's unique, it's English. It's slightly mysterious because nobody really knows where these places are. It takes you into a faraway place that you can't really comprehend unless you're one of these people bobbing up and down in the Channel.'

Zeb Soanes, a regular Shipping Forecast reader, says, 'To the non-nautical, it's a nightly litany of the sea. It reinforces a sense of being islanders with a proud seafaring past. Whilst the listener is safely tucked-up in their bed, they can imagine small fishing-boats sailing at Plymouth or 170ft waves crashing against Rockall.'

Another regular reader of the forecast, Kathy Clugston, describes it as 'like a lullaby'. Jo Ellison of the *Financial Times* wrote that 'it's a beloved cultural icon, a tacit expression of our national identity.'

The forecast hints at the vastness of the sea and the unknown, conjuring images of distant, unseen places. For listeners, there is a sense of vicarious adventure in hearing about weather conditions in remote parts of the ocean, sparking the imagination and evoking the romance and danger of maritime life.

The Shipping Forecast airs when people are winding down or just waking up. The calm, reassuring voice delivering the forecast at these quiet, reflective times can trigger deep emotions, offering a connection to the wider world or a moment of peaceful solitude. It is prayer-like.

Art forms

The forecast has inspired artists in music, literature and television.

The band Radiohead sampled the Shipping Forecast in their song '*The National Anthem*' from the album *Kid A*. The abstract, disjointed nature of the forecast added to the song's atmosphere of anxiety and disorientation.

In his '*Glanmore Sonnets, VII*', Nobel Laureate Seamus Heaney uses words from the broadcast, blending its calming presence with themes of uncertainty and danger, adding vivid phrases like 'Sirens of the tundra' - evoking the beckoning mysteries of cold, unforgiving landscapes.

In his 2005 documentary '*Incomplete & Utter History of Classical Music,*' Stephen Fry highlighted the forecast's importance in British culture and its unique, musical qualities.

17th October 2024

63 Abraham

The Abraham Accords

'Thy name shall be Abraham. A father of many nations have I made thee.'

- Genesis, 17:5

The *Abraham Accords* are peace agreements on Arab–Israeli co-operation and peace that were signed between Israel and the United Arab Emirates and between Israel and Bahrain in September, 2020.

The agreements recognised Israel's sovereignty, enabling the establishment of full diplomatic relations. This allowed the 'normalisation' of trade, flights, tourism and the lifting of travel bureaucracy soon followed.

Israel's initial agreement with the UAE marked the first instance of Israel establishing diplomatic relations with an Arab country since 1994, when the Israel–Jordan peace treaty came into effect.

The agreements were named Abraham Accords to highlight the common belief of Judaism and Islam in the prophet Abraham.

On October 23rd, 2020, Israel and Sudan agreed to normalise ties, and as part of the agreement, the United States removed Sudan from its list of state sponsors of terrorism and giving it a US$1.2 billion loan.

When the Israel–Morocco normalisation agreement was signed, in exchange for Morocco's recognition of Israeli sovereignty, the US recognised Moroccan sovereignty over Western Sahara.

In January 2020, President Trump announced the peace plan for the Middle East with Israeli prime minister Benjamin Netanyahu. The plan provided for a unified Jerusalem as Israel's capital and Israeli sovereignty over the Jordan Valley and the principal Jewish settlements in the West Bank, amounting to annexation of roughly 30% of the territory. The Palestinians would get desert areas near the Egyptian border, sovereignty, and a non-contiguous state with numerous Israeli enclaves.

The *New York Times* wrote that 'rather than viewing it as a serious blueprint for peace, analysts called it a political document by a president in the middle of an impeachment trial working in tandem with Mr. Netanyahu, a prime minister under criminal indictment who is about to face his third election in a year'.

Saudi

Saudi Arabia considers itself the leader of the Islamic world, a status rooted in its custodianship of the two holiest sites in Islam, Mecca and Medina.

Saudi Arabia's *Vision 2030* plan aims to reduce the kingdom's reliance on oil and gas by diversifying its economy. Normalising relations with Israel could open up opportunities for advanced technology partnerships, particularly in sectors like cybersecurity, agriculture, and water management. The UAE and Bahrain have already reaped economic benefits from their involvement in the Abraham Accords, which could motivate Saudi Arabia to follow suit.

Saudi Arabia and Israel share a common concern regarding Iran's growing influence in the Middle East, especially its nuclear ambitions and its support for proxy groups across the region. A formal alliance with Israel could strengthen Saudi Arabia's security posture, providing access to advanced Israeli defence technologies and intelligence-sharing against common threats.

Emirates

While Israel and the UAE had long-maintained de facto recognition in areas of business including the diamond trade and the high tech industries of artificial intelligence and defence, the accord opened the door to a much wider range of economic investments.

A number of Israeli and UAE law firms and healthcare providers announced collaborations. Lishot, an Israeli water quality testing company was the first Israeli firm making deliveries to Dubai.

A number of kosher restaurants were opened in the UAE to cater to Jewish visitors. Abu Dhabi Investment Office opened its first overseas branch in Israel. UAE businesses began acquiring stakes in Israeli assets, such as Beitar Jerusalem football team, Haifa Port Company, and Israir Airlines.

According to Israel's Ministry of Defence, the value of Israeli defence exports to countries with which it normalised relations in 2020 reached $791 million.

22nd September 2024

XII – Society

'I would rather be governed by the first 2,000 people in the Boston telephone directory, than by the 2,000 people on the faculty of Harvard University.'

– William F. Buckley

64 North

Where Greggs meets Pret

The north-south divide

Some say it's at the Watford Gap services. Others say it's at the Severn-Wash line. But isn't the true marker of arrival in 'the North' the moment you reach a place where you can't get a smashed avocado and roasted pepper baguette, but can get an impressive variety of sausage rolls?

That is the contention of mathematicians who have calculated the location where southern *Pret a Manger* sandwiches ends and the rule of honest, northern *Greggs* pies begins – and they have declared it as the *north-south divide*.

Lest the analysis seems flimsy, they have strengthened it by augmenting it with a separate set of strongly correlated data: the *Waitrose-Morrisons* Index.

As far as Sophie Maclean, from *King's College London*, is concerned, this study ends a discussion that began with William the Conqueror, who noticed that the residents in the north of his kingdom were more unruly and, 'in mad fury ... descended on the English of the north like a raging lion.'

'There's a lot of debate, but thankfully mathematicians have worked this out,' said Maclean, speaking at the Cheltenham Science Festival. 'Really there is only one way to judge what's North and what's South and that is by looking at the distribution of *Pret* and *Greggs*.'

The analysis, published in journal *ArXiv*, used Machine Learning to define the optimal north-south boundary, seeking to divide the country in two according to the ratio of *Prets* to *Greggs* and, separately, *Waitroses* to *Morrisons*. Then, researchers combined the two.

This produced a line that cut off the top of Norfolk and all of Cornwall and Bristol, thereby declaring that these traditionally southern regions are in fact spiritually and culinarily northern.

Part of this may be explained by the metric failing in the west country. While most of the country has a dominance of one of the fast-food chains or another, Cornwall is fairly low on *Prets*, possibly on socioeconomic grounds, but the region also resists *Greggs*, on grounds of '*pasty-purism*.'

Less controversially, further east, the line confirmed conventional intuition – passing close to the Watford Gap.

Dr Robin Smith, from Sheffield Hallam University, led the study, adapting machine learning techniques normally used to look at nuclear reactions. He said that in an inevitably subjective area, this analysis was as good as any. 'The food we eat is a very good indicator of whether someone is northern or southern. *Greggs* is very popular in the north, where people do seem to prefer a steak bake.'

The new definition will undoubtedly trigger some discomfort. Cheltenham residents, who like little better than meeting on a Saturday morning in Waitrose to pick up 'essential' parmigiano reggiano, might at the very least argue the case they are an enclave of the south.

Maclean accepts that there will be controversies, disagreements and some anomalies. The same goes for any other purportedly objective measure. There was even sometimes a pathos to the data, where you can see the anomalies in action – for instance, in the few individuals trying to eke out a sophisticated culinary lifestyle amid the pastry-based wastelands of the north.

'You could imagine the single *Pret* in Newcastle surrounded by a swarm of *Greggs*,' Maclean said. Whereas, she added, 'In London, they say you're never more than 6m from a rat, or a Pret.'

Greggs has begun a southern invasion, with an appeal to more liberal metropolitan tastes. 'Since *Greggs* produced the vegan sausage roll, it has become more popular in the south, so this might not be a marker of *northernness* for that much longer.'

31st August 2023

65 Cabals

Cabals and modern prejudice

Billionaires are not the problem

There was a non-story in *The Times* newspaper on 9th August 2023 reporting that the world's 5th richest man, Larry Ellison, founder of the technology firm *Oracle*, was 'bankrolling' Tony Blair's think-tank, the *Institute for Global Change*.

So what? There is another name for this: transparency.

When Arron Banks donates to the UKIP / Brexit / Reform, that's known as 'financing'. But when it's a Tony Blair initiative, it's 'bankrolling'.

There is a distasteful tradition, going back centuries, of randomly choosing a distinct group of people and ascribing the ills of the world to them. The assertion is that if we somehow removed these people, then life would be magically fairer.

Throughout history, the notion of secretive groups exerting control over society has been a recurring theme. These groups, often referred to as '*cabals,*' have ignited conspiracy theories, bred mistrust, and fuelled prejudices against various communities.

It really doesn't matter who '*they*' are: it could be ethnic minorities, immigrants, 'elites', 'the Establishment'. But equally it could also be: pharmaceutical companies, the *Rothchilds*, oil companies, white men, the *World Economic Forum* or billionaires.

Historical cabals

Cabals, characterised by their secretive nature and alleged influence over political, economic, and social affairs, originally referred to a small group of advisers. It gained prominence during the 17th century in England, with the 'Cabal Ministry' of Charles II and the alleged 'Illuminati' conspiracy during the Enlightenment. These suspicions arise in times of political turmoil, uncertainty, or social change.

The unemployment, inflation, and hunger in Germany after the First World War was exploited by Adolf Hitler in his beer-hall speeches on 'the Jewish problem'. This escalated to create the populist movement known as National Socialism.

Bigotry begins at home

Prejudices often emerge when individuals or groups are scapegoated for perceived unfairness or economic disparities. Minority populations, including racial and religious minorities, have been falsely accused of conspiratorial control, deflecting attention from the real, systemic problems.

Similarly, the rise of anti-Semitic sentiment, fuelled by baseless conspiracy theories, reflects historical accusations against Jews for manipulating global events, by allegedly controlling the media, banking, and Hollywood. And at the same time being behind International Socialism. Can it be both? Make up your minds.

In the case of billionaires, their 'disproportionate' power can lead to resentment and bitterness. The concentration of wealth and influence in the hands of a few can foster belief that these individuals control economies and governments, akin to cabals of the past.

Immigrants, too, have been vilified as a perceived threat, often falsely accused of undermining cultures, despite their vital contributions. In the UK, legal immigrants account for 11% of the population but they contribute 13% to the nation's income. I wonder how long this surplus will last, though.

The future of an illusion

While historical and modern prejudices target different groups, they share a common misconception: the belief that *external forces* control individual lives. This illusion can lead to misplaced blame, and a sense of powerlessness. In reality, each individual retains agency over their own life choices and decisions. Modern prejudices stem from a fear of losing autonomy to these perceived cabals, neglecting the power of personal responsibility.

To combat the harmful effects of prejudice, it is essential to recognise the historical patterns of cabalistic suspicions so that we can dismantle these baseless conspiracy theories. Through open dialogue and debate we can understand the complexities behind the formidable problems we face, and avoid scapegoating specific groups.

Education plays a key role in dispelling myths and encouraging individuals to take accountability for their actions. Empowerment comes from realising that '*those people over there*' don't actually control our lives. We do.

22nd February 2024

66 Guns

Guns and poses

'Tradition is not the worship of ashes, but the preservation of fire.'
- Gustav Mahler

Ritual and ceremony

Jordan Peterson, the psychologist, in a live debate in Vancouver with Sam Harris, the cognitive neuroscientist, said that he tried to live *'as if God exists.'*

Harris then described a vivid and connected example of metaphorical and literal truths.

Anyone who has worked with guns at all has heard the admonishment to 'treat every gun as if it is loaded.'

'If I had a gun here that I wanted to show you,' says Harris, 'and if I know anything about guns, I'm going to make damned sure that it's unloaded. I'm going to drop the magazine, pull back the slide, check the chamber. And do this in a redundant fashion that really looks like I'm suffering from obsessive compulsive disorder.

And then I'll hand it to you. And if you know anything about guns, you will do the same thing, *having just seen me do it*. And if you hand it back to me, again, I will do the same thing. Even though there may be no ammunition around. It really is crazy at the level of our explicit knowledge of the situation, and yet, absolutely necessary to do. And it runs very deep. That whole time, you're careful not to point the barrel of the gun at anything you would be afraid to shoot. And when people fail to live this way around guns, they, with some unnerving frequency, actually shoot themselves or people close to them, by accident.

So it's really the only proper hedge against the odds of being in proximity to loaded weapons.

And yet, if someone came up to us in the middle of this operation, and said 'there's a casino that just opened across the street that will take your bets about whether or not the gun is loaded. Would you like to bet a million dollars as to whether or not this gun is loaded?' Well, of course, I would bet those million dollars every time that it's not loaded, because I know it's not loaded.

There is a literal truth and a metaphorical truth - otherwise known as a very *useful fiction*. Which, in this case, is *actually more useful than the truth*. But the only way I can understand its utility is in the context of distinguishing metaphorical truth from literal truth.

This all works while there is no casino. But when the casino opens you do want some purchase on the literal truth. But it's a viscerally real experience. If I have a real gun that I know to be unloaded, I still emotionally cannot treat it as a harmless object. I can't point it at my child just for the fun of it - we can't play cops and robbers now with a real gun.

I have a superstitious attachment to *always being safe*, with the gun. And it's important that this gets ingrained. It's not strictly rational. It's not irrational because it has good effects, but it's not in register with what I know to be true factually.

This is low cost. It's not dividing societies or causing war.'

Peterson concludes, 'This whole story transforms itself from something that's enacted out as a dramatic ritual into a psychological reality. Let's say you own an antique. It's valuable. And you think, I'm going to take this antique apart, and I'm going to find out *where* the value is. Good luck! The value is a social agreement about its position in a hierarchy. Nothing to do with its material substance.'

15th February 2024

67 Now II

We have formidable challenges in 2023.

We have a rising cost of living. We have young people who cannot accrue capital, but are nevertheless expected to become capitalists. A housing crisis where targets for house building are never met. We have an era where automation is taking away blue collar jobs, and A.I. is taking away white collar jobs.

And yet we are focused on noise. On frivolous formulas and corporate obsessions.

True story: I was once denied a promotion because I wasn't a woman. The metrics, ratios and quotas were running against me. This was official policy. Then, when I eventually did get that promotion, whenever I was on stage, on a speaking panel, there was one particular female executive who would perennially question why it was '*always* middle-aged white men on the stage.'

My usual answer was to quote the impressive diversity statistics in the new graduate intake. But we all knew that as the new young women progressed in the firm, at some point *some* of them would choose to have children, and pause their ascension up the ranks. This would 'distort' the numbers again.

Camile Paglia, professor at Philadelphia University, suggests that all civilisations and empires become obsessed with gender at the declining end of their powerful reigns - Egyptian, Chinese, Greek, Roman, Byzantine, Ottoman. They begin inventing opaque, oblique and obtuse questions.

We are there once again. Men's right to have babies, as predicted by Stan/Lauretta in *The Life of Brian*, being a 'symbolic struggle against reality.'

'We are distracted from distraction by distraction,' said T.S. Eliot.

Then there's the current trend to delay things, until conditions are 'optimal'. We often hear, 'I need to find love', 'a partner', 'a home', 'a promotion' - whatever it is. 'I don't want to do anything else until these things are sorted for me'. It's an extremely common complaint from young people.

A suggested answer, came 64 years ago.

In 1939, C. S. Lewis gave a speech at the university church of St Mary the Virgin, in Oxford. He said: -

'Human life has always been lived on the edge of a precipice. Human culture has always had to exist under the shadow of something infinitely more important than itself. If man had postponed the search for knowledge and beauty until they were secure, the search would never have begun.

Life has never been normal. Even those periods which we think most tranquil, like the nineteenth century, turn out on closer inspection to be full of crises, alarms, difficulties, emergencies.

Plausible reasons have never been lacking for putting off all merely cultural activities until some imminent danger has been averted, or some crying injustice put right. But humanity long ago chose to neglect those plausible reasons.

They wanted knowledge and beauty, and they wanted them now. And they would not wait for the suitable moment that never comes.

The Athens of Pericles, leaves us not only the Parthenon, but significantly *The Funeral Oration*.

The insects have chosen a different line. They have sought first the material welfare and the security of the hive. And presumably, they can enjoy their reward.

But men, men are different. They propound mathematical theorems in beleaguered cities. They conduct metaphysical arguments in condemned cells. Make jokes on scaffolds. Discuss the last new poem whilst advancing to the walls of Quebec. And comb their hair, at the gates of Thermopylae.

This is not panache. It is our nature.'

A call to arms, in less favourable times.

16th November 2023

68 Britain

A progressive mission

The UK state is spending more than ever before, except in times of war or crisis, and taxing more, but with poor outcomes. Waiting lists for health treatment have trebled since 2010, this generation is half as likely as the last to be homeowners by the age of 30, and two million children receive free school meals, which is a third above the long-term average. The average UK worker has received no real pay rise since 2007. Today, the over 50s hold 78% of the housing wealth.

All the G7 countries (USA, Germany, France, UK, Italy, Japan, Canada), representing a third of global wealth, suffered declines in growth and productivity since the 2009 financial crisis. But Britian has fallen the most. Brexit has had a significant impact. Foreign Direct Investment inflows the UK are at their lowest levels since the 1980s.

The state has not kept pace with the world's demographic and technological changes. Over the last 30 years, spending on social care has risen faster than on transport, spending on pensions has risen more than housing and research and development combined. Health spending has increased by

£165 billion, but only £6 billion of that has been on capital investment.

The pressures will grow. We will have another 4 million elderly in the next twenty years.

The good news

Technology has changed the private sector. In 2003, three of the world's 10 largest companies were in technology (*Microsoft, Intel* and *IBM*). Today, it's 8 of the 10 (*Apple, Microsoft, Amazon, Tesla, Meta, Alphabet, NVIDIA,* and *Taiwan Semiconductors*). The only non-techs are *Berkshire Hathaway* (Warren Buffet's investment firm) and *Saudi Aramco* (the world's largest oil producer).

Research and development spending by these tech giants exceeds that of governments'. *Amazon* spends three times more on R&D than the UK.

Acceleration is inevitable, but the state has been slow to adopt data analytics, AI and cloud computing. Two examples: furlough support during Covid cost £70 billion, and household support in the energy price crisis cost £40 billion. Both are huge *untargeted* interventions. Technology-enabled targeting, allowing those most in need to receive the funds, would have saved 70% and 25% respectively.

Britain has huge advantages: world class universities, the largest finance sector in Europe, it's 3rd behind the US and China in venture capital, and the leader in Europe for A.I. talent.

Conditions for growth

Ryan Wain, executive director at the *Institute for Global Change,* suggests some compelling recommendations.

Firstly, redesign the planning laws. It takes *four years* to gain planning permission for major infrastructure projects (this has doubled over the last ten years). *Crossrail* – the *Elizabeth* line – was 4 years late and £4 billion over budget. In housing, 4 out of 5 planning applications are delayed by 2 years. High-speed Internet has not been delivered at the pace needed.

We need a high speed and agile planning process: a 6-month maximum deadline for planning approvals.

Second, address labour shortages: allow migration for key occupations like construction and hospitality for EU citizens, at zero cost and zero bureaucracy. There are 1.1 million job vacancies in Britain today, leaving the economy £39 billion worse off annually. That's 26% more vacancies than the same period pre-Brexit.

Key sectors suffer: construction experiences a 36% increase in vacancies, hospitality 30%, and health and social work 39%. These industries blame Brexit for their challenges. We have the highest on-record migration, yet we have significant labour shortages.

Mastering and harnessing the 21st century's technological revolution is our new progressive political mission.

18th January 2024

69 Oikophilia

The love of home

Oikos, from which we take our word *economy,* is a Greek word which means the household, the order and guidance of a home.

It is the private world of a person's abode. Also of a family, but by extension also of a village, a people, or an ethnicity.

Oikophilia is a principle of value for the small, the local, and the private.

The most important things people build, even more important than the cathedrals and great works of art and music, are not primarily the result of planning. They develop organically over time, with trial and error, as the work of many hands. An example is the Common Law of England.

Recognising this, we seek to protect these things against those who would tear them down out of a misguided zeal for what they see as the demands of liberty, equality, or social justice.

In the Judeo-Christian tradition, the concept of love of home has deep roots in the fabric of religious and cultural identity. The Hebrew Bible is full of stories that emphasise a sacred land. It is not only a geographic space but a symbol of covenant and identity.

Similarly, in Christianity, the concept of home transcends the physical world. The New Testament emphasises a spiritual dimension to belonging. This communal bond extends beyond familial ties to encompass a broader community united by shared values.

Contemporary populist intolerance threatens to erode the foundations of oikophilia. The relentless pursuit of individualism, and the divisive nature of populist movements overshadow the inherent value of love for one's home and community. The workplace, instead of being a space for collaboration and shared purpose, has become a battleground for power struggles.

Oikophilia originates in our need for nurture and safety, and is a call to responsibility.

We can define some core characteristics of oikophilia: respect for the dead, community connection, the voice of tradition, aesthetic local appreciation, and natural piety or respect for the sacred.

Green philosophy, motivated by Edmund Burke's concept of trusteeship, encompassing the dead and the unborn, our responsibility to past and future generations, combined with a love of home, offers a natural incentive to preserve our local habitat.

The motive in oikophilia is the love of country, love of territory and love of that territory as home. It is a natural motive that can act as a catalyst in reversing environmental degradation. Only at the local level will people find a genuinely motivating force to preserve what they identify as theirs, unlike the apocalyptic visions of environmentalism.

UK Green Party politician Caroline Lucas is critical of this idea. Lucas sees oikophilia as desirable, but doubts its practicality, and argues that the idea that a volunteering spirit emanating from a love of home will solve global environmental issues is pure fantasy.

Animosity towards state and central power stems from a broad suspicion of top-down, big government and its disposition to ignore unintended consequences or undesirable side-effects of its decision making. Instead, it is claimed, environmental degradation can be tackled from the bottom-up through community groups, local organisations and civic associations. One such civil association is the *Women's Institute*, which 'has no other purpose than to encourage its members to gather around socially beneficial projects' (Roger Scruton).

The fast emerging field of Geo-engineering, particularly the practice of carbon capture, is one radical development that gives us ammunition and armour for the cause. There is evidence of its cost effectiveness and immediate impact.

The benefits of large-scale, transnational schemes like geo-engineering is an admission that oikophilia alone is not a powerful enough tool to fight global issues like climate change.

29th February 2024

70 Habits

'The vice of Capitalism is the unequal sharing of blessings. The virtue of Socialism is the equal sharing of misery.'

– Winston Churchill

Does inequality kill?

Take the London Underground train eastwards from Green Park on the Jubilee line, and the average life expectancy for someone born in London drops by one year for every two stops.

If you travel northbound from Hyde Park Corner to Holloway Road, a fifteen minute ride on the Piccadilly line, life expectancy decreases by eleven years.

Along London Underground lines, there are large income differences, but the causality is contested. Income is often less important than the lifestyle it is associated with. Those who lack education smoke more, eat more unhealthily, and exercise less but it is not because they have less money.

Cigarettes are expensive but you can take a walk for free. A major reason for differences in life expectancy is that smoking is four times more common in the most deprived areas of England than those living in the least deprived areas.

These differences are more related to the fact that it has become a status symbol in the middle and upper class to exercise, think about diet and live a healthy life. It has become embarrassing not to take care of oneself, and social stigma means such habits spread fast.

There is one thing that seems to work in changing people's habits. In 2016, American researchers in the *Journal of the American Medical Association* discovered that low income earners have better health if they live in cities with many high income earners.

Seeing people with higher incomes and better housing every day was assumed to make one 'status stressed', humiliated and ill. But it turns out it makes one feel better and live longer than being surrounded by people of the same income level. You exercise more, smoke less, and are less likely to suffer from obesity.

Why? Habits are contagious. Working out has a positive impact.

Case Study

In 1999, Venezuelan president Hugo Chavez and his disciple Nicholas Maduro initiated a policy of nationalisation and massive state spending. They had vast oil reserves and a national income of 1,000 billion dollars, that kept their policy afloat for many years.

Bernie Sanders said that the 'American Dream was more alive in Venezuela than in the US'. In an open letter to

Chavez, stars of the Left, such as Naomi Klein, Jesse Jackson and Howard Zinn, said they 'see Venezuela as a model of how a country's wealth can benefit all its people.'

On paper, that 1,000 billion dollars was enough to make every extremely poor individual in Venezuela a millionaire. But it's not much money if you do not invest it productively.

There then followed one of the worst economist disasters to have occurred anywhere in the world in peace time.

Between 2010 and 2020, Venezuela's average income plummeted by 75%. South America's richest country suddenly became South America's poorest, with bread lines and an exodus from an increasingly tyrannical state. Around 7m Venezuelans fled the country (25% of the population).

Since then, Venezuela hasn't been mentioned as a beacon of hope.

Efficiency and productivity

The economist Milton Friedman was on a foreign speaking tour. Stuck in traffic due to roadworks, he asked his host why the workers in the street were using shovels, instead of machinery. The answer was that it was a deliberate government policy, in order maintain employment levels.

Friedman retorted, 'Then why don't you give them spoons instead of shovels, and create even more jobs?

20th June 2024

71 Revolutions

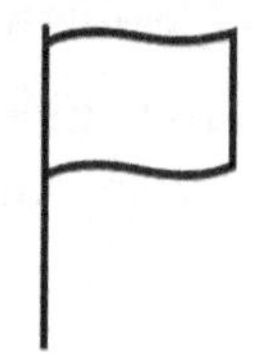

'By all means have your revolution. But then, having had it, change nothing for twenty years.'

– Peter Brooke

Two revolutions, both alike in dignity, in Paris and Athens, where we lay our scene. One changed absolutely nothing, and the other changed the whole of Europe.

The French revolution of 1789 overthrew King Louis XVI, to replace monarchy with dictatorship.

'After two hundred years, there is no more aristocratic country than France. Nothing has changed,' said the late Professor George Steiner, who grew up in the competitive French education system, before and after the Second World War.

In 1821, the Greek revolutionaries overthrew their Ottoman rulers to create modern day Greece.

Professor Roderick Beaton, of King's College London, has emphasised the significant impact of the Greek Revolution of 1821 in several key ways. He argues that the revolution was pivotal for Greece but also had international implications. According to Beaton, the Greek Revolution marked a shift from a Europe dominated by multinational empires to one of nation-states. The international recognition of Greece as a sovereign nation, formalised by the Protocol of London in 1830, was a critical moment in this transition and has been largely overlooked by historians.

In essence, Beaton views the Greek Revolution as a key event that contributed to the reshaping of Europe into a continent of independent nations, influencing geopolitical developments well beyond its time.

France

Despite the revolutionary ideals of equality, the French Revolution failed to significantly address social inequality. The aristocracy was replaced by a new ruling class, and disparities between the rich and poor persisted.

The violent excesses of the Reign of Terror, led by lawyer and statesman Maximilien Robespierre, resulted in widespread fear and loss of life without achieving substantial long-term change. Instead, it led to instability and a backlash against its ideals.

The revolution eventually gave way to the rise of Napoleon Bonaparte, who established himself as a dictator and restored authoritarian rule. Thus, the revolution did not lead to lasting democratic reforms.

The revolutionary upheaval disrupted the economy, leading to periods of financial instability and hardship for many ordinary citizens. Despite aspirations for economic justice, the revolution did not bring about sustainable economic improvement for all.

While the revolution resulted in the end of absolute monarchy in France, it did not change the nature of monarchical rule in Europe. Monarchies persisted across the continent, limiting the revolution's broader impact on governance structures.

Greece

In contrast to France, the Greek Revolution of 1821 was the most permanent and influential uprising of the last 200 years and it moulded modern Europe.

The Greek Revolution was one of the earliest successful nationalist uprisings in Europe, inspiring other ethnic groups under foreign rule to seek independence and self-determination. It set a precedent for nationalist movements throughout the 19th and 20th centuries, ultimately leading to the dissolution of empires and the creation of nation-states.

The Greek Revolution sparked a renewed interest in classical Greek culture across Europe. The philhellenic movement attracted intellectuals, artists, and activists who saw Greece as the cradle of Western civilisation. This cultural revival had a profound impact on European art, literature, and politics.

Greece's success reshaped the geopolitical landscape of Europe, weakening the Ottoman Empire and created a resurgence of Greek status. This realignment of power contributed to the decline of Turkish-Ottoman influence in the region.

With significant international support, many volunteers from various European countries joined the struggle and raised awareness of the Greek cause. This marked one of the earliest instances of humanitarian intervention in modern history, setting a precedent for future interventions to support oppressed peoples.

1st August 2024

72 Election

'Romeo is banished'

– Prince Escalus, *Romeo and Juliet*

This coming General Election, on the 4th of July, 2024, will be my tenth.

10th Election Special: the pros and cons of each party.

Conservative

For: Free market belief. Individual freedom. Free speech. Low taxes. Low government intervention. Personal responsibility, and accountability. Not blaming others. Spending own money, not other people's. Community foundations. Pride in country. Support for military. Fiscal prudence, not spending beyond our means. Most inclusive party without any overt bias. Three women PMs. A black chancellor. An Indian PM. Labour are nowhere near this. The black chancellor was terrible, but it's about meritocracy, so when he was found out, he was fired. More inclined to support Israel. More supportive of UK oil and gas production. It's still needed. Believe more in trade and innovation rather than regulation.

Against: This is the first Parliament in modern history during which living standards have fallen. Debt at its highest rate in 60 years, with debt interest payments being the fastest growing area of government spending. NHS waiting lists at 7.5 million. Schools and hospitals are crumbling. Huge rise in use of food-banks. Not executed on *'levelling up'*. Many communities left behind. London centric. Rest of country not seen as relevant. Self-centred. Selfish. Have not delivered on immigration controls. Corruption and lack of standards in public life. Allowed Johnson free rein, who is a judicially proven liar. Insufficient belief in European trade. Have run core institutions into the ground – NHS, BBC, Civil Service, Foreign Office, the courts, the countryside. We are low on civic pride. They don't believe in arts funding. Regulatory capture. Too cosy with the City and big business. Dangerous influence of venture capitalists and *Singapore-on-Thames* freeport ideas. Posh boys who thought it would be fun to run the country for a while.

They need a long banishment.

Conclusion: 0% chance of voting Conservative.

Labour

For: Sounding serious on economics and business. Let's see. Some impressive individuals. Yvette Cooper. Lisa Nandy. Sensible thinking on levelling up and regional economic support. More pro-Europe as a trading bloc. Fairness. Fewer vested interests – fewer dodgy business connections. Maurice Glasman influence and *Blue Labour* movement – connecting to communities and localism. Investment in trades, apprenticeships, skills and services. More inclined to support the arts.

Against: More in favour of government intervention and interference in markets. More in favour of nationalised industry - energy or rail or water. The problem with this is that they won't have the best talent, and it distorts the market. Labour is captured by trade unions, and held hostage by them. Some unimpressive MPs. Vestiges of pre-historic Corbynista relics. Apologising for heritage and inheritance. They wobble when asked what a woman is. Too lenient on Hamas. Not sufficiently steely on immigration. Not financially competent – see Birmingham council bankruptcy. Anti UK oil and gas production. Think more about regulation than trade. Insufficient clout on innovation. New Marxists are too influential – Aaron Bastani and *Novara Media* (they're suspicious con-artists). Keir Starmer once knocked on my door. When I asked him about Cyprus and pressure on Turkey, he froze.

Conclusion: 99.9% chance of voting Labour. Buyer's remorse will inevitably follow, but it's the only rational choice for now.

Liberal Democrats: Nothing to say.

Green Party: I don't believe in agricultural feudalism. They don't believe in technology, trade, growth, and individual freedom. I agree with them on civic pride, localism, restraint, stewardship, and ecological custodianship.

My 10 Election voting history, since you asked so nicely

1987: Gremloids Party (Lord Buckethead). 1992: Conservative (John Major). 1997: Liberal Democrat (Paddy Ashdown). 2001: Labour (Tony Blair). 2005: Labour (Tony Blair). 2010: Labour (Gordon Brown). 2015: Labour (Ed Miliband). 2017: Conservative (Theresa May). 2019: Liberal Democrat (Jo Swinson). 2024: Labour (Sir Keir Starmer).

Vote early. Vote often.

30th May 2024

73 Fact

'In fact' – from Prospect magazine

Oxford University is 300 years older than the Aztec Empire.

The rock band Aerosmith have made more money in royalties from the video game *Guitar Hero: Aerosmith* than from any of their albums.

Windscreen wipers, laser printers and bulletproof vests were invented by women.

Queen Cleopatra lived closer to the invention of the iPhone than she did to the construction of the Pyramids.

1 person in 10 in the world relies on the river Ganges for water.

In the Eskimo language Inuktitut, there is a word meaning 'I should try not to become an alcoholic' - Imminngernaveersaartunngortussaavunga.

Paul Newman was number 19 on Richard Nixon's enemies list.

Britain is now the only major country in the world in which French is the main foreign language taught in schools.

In the James Bond movies, a third of the women who sleep with Bond end up dead. Daniel Craig is the most dangerous 007 to sleep with.

Each year, between 30,000 and 80,000 meteorites land on earth.

Since signing for Liverpool, Mohamed Salah has received more yellow cards from celebrating goals against Manchester United at Anfield, than Manchester United have scored goals at Anfield.

Of India's 1.4 billion population, only 63 million pay tax (that's 4.5%).

Honey never spoils. Archaeologists have found pots of honey in ancient Egyptian tombs that are over 3,000 years old, and are still edible.

A day on Venus is longer than a year on Venus*.

The shortest war in history was between Britain and Zanzibar on August 27, 1896. Zanzibar surrendered after 38 minutes.

There is a city called Rome on every single continent.

Cows form close friendships, but they can also hold grudges for years.

Winter lasts for 21 years on Uranus.

A piece of chewing gum costs on average 5p, and 10p to remove from the pavement.

People born in December are the most likely to make a claim on car insurance.

90% of China's and Russia's billionaires are children of communist party officials.

Half of all bank robberies take place on a Friday.

An amputated newt limb will grow back fully within ten weeks.

Happiness peaks at the age of 74. The lowest point is age 40.

No word in the English language rhymes with month, orange*, silver or purple.

Toy weapons are now included in 30% of LEGO sets.

Over the next two decades, China will construct as many new buildings as Europe's total current stock.

In 1971, a third of Britons over 16 had no teeth; in 2004, this fell to just 12 per cent.

In 2003, the Welsh assembly achieved parity in members between men and women - the first democratically elected chamber in the world to do so.

Before World War I the Home Office employed 28 people. It now employs 35,000.

Half of all Australians will contract skin cancer at some point in their lives.

Apple has created 5 million jobs in China, about twice the number of jobs it has created and supported in the US.

Sharks have existed for over 400 million years, predating dinosaurs. They have survived five mass extinctions, showing their adaptability and resilience.

Saturn's north pole features a unique hexagon-shaped storm, about 32,000 kilometres wide. The storm has persisted for decades and remains a natural mystery.

** - 243 Earth days for one rotation on its axis (a day), and 225 Earth days for one orbit around the sun (a year).*

*** - Eminem disagrees. With the right intonation he has made orange rhyme with George, storage, door hinge, four-inch, porridge, foreign, and syringe.*

28th September 2024

74 Overton

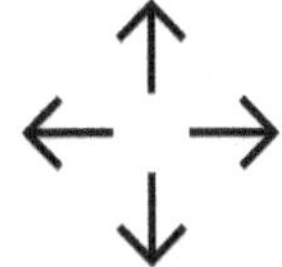

What is the 'Overton Window'?

'Small changes are the causes of great ones.'
- Aristotle

The *Overton window* is a theory that describes the range of previously unthinkable ideas that become *acceptable* or *mainstream* at a given time.

Named after political analyst Joseph Overton (1960 - 2003), the window represents the range of what is politically viable - acceptable, sensible, or even popular. And ideas outside this window are considered too extreme or radical. Votes for women (1918), and same-sex marriage (2014), spring to mind.

Politicians often work within the Overton window to propose policies that will gain public support. Alternatively, they may try to shift the window itself, making previously suspect ideas more acceptable over time.

Examples of the Overton window

Legalisation of marijuana: In the 20th century, the idea of legalising marijuana for recreational use was far outside the Overton window in most countries. It was seen as too extreme and dangerous. In recent years, there has been a significant shift in public opinion, driven by changes in attitudes toward drug use, some documented successes of medical marijuana, and growing recognition of the social costs of prohibition. As a result, several US states and countries like Canada have legalised marijuana for recreational use, moving the idea well within the window.

Universal Basic Income (UBI): The concept of a *Universal Basic Income*, where the government provides a regular, unconditional payment to all citizens, was once considered an outlandish idea. But due to rising concerns about automation, job displacement, and economic inequality, UBI has moved much closer to the mainstream. Pilot programmes and serious political discussions have made it more acceptable to consider. While still controversial, UBI is now within the Overton window in many places, where it is discussed as a viable policy option.

Immigration: In the early 2000s, immigration was largely viewed through the lens of economic benefit, with the Labour government under Tony Blair promoting policies that welcomed migrants, particularly from the newly expanded European Union. Immigration was considered a positive force for economic growth, and restrictive immigration policies were seen as less acceptable within the mainstream discourse.

By the mid-2000s to early 2010s public concern about the impact of immigration grew, particularly in relation to pressures on public services, jobs, and cultural integration. The issue moved closer to the centre of the political debate. Increasing media focus on immigration issues reflected and contributed to this shift. After 2010, The Conservative Party, under David Cameron, adopted stricter immigration policies, promising to reduce net migration to 'tens of thousands' annually. The issue of immigration became increasingly central to political discourse, with public concern driving policy proposals that were previously considered too restrictive.

This shift was instrumental in the Brexit referendum campaign, where immigration control was a key issue.

Automation and the future of work: Originally, discussions about AI were mostly focused on theoretical or technical aspects, with little mainstream concern about automation's impact on jobs. The idea that AI could significantly disrupt employment was considered speculative and outside the Overton window.

As AI technologies began to mature and be applied in various industries, the conversation shifted. Concerns about job displacement, the gig economy, and the need for retraining workers moved into the mainstream. Reports from think tanks, policymakers, and business leaders brought these issues to the forefront.

Today, the impact of AI on employment is a central issue in political discourse, with discussions about training, managing the transition, protecting workers, and ensuring that AI benefits are broadly shared. Related debates over universal basic income, lifelong learning, and new social safety nets illustrate how these ideas have moved within the Overton window.

30th December 2024

XIII - Greeks

Αεί ο θεός ο μέγας γεωμετρεί το σύμπαν.

God always applies geometry to the universe.

— Plato

75 Diogenes

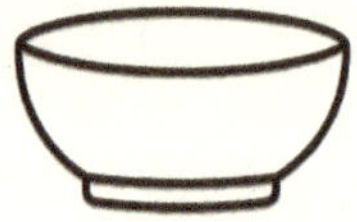

Ten lessons from Diogenes the Cynic

Άνθρωπον ζητώ
'I am searching for an honest man.'
– Diogenes of Sinope

The Dog

Diogenes the Cynic was a Greek philosopher who lived in the 4th century BCE. Known for his wildly eccentric and unconventional behaviour, he embraced a minimalist lifestyle and challenged the social rules of his time.

Diogenes was born in Sinope, a Greek colony on the Black Sea coast. He was a student of Antisthenes, the founder of Cynicism, a philosophical school that emphasised self-sufficiency and the rejection of material possessions.

Diogenes became the most famous Cynic philosopher of his time, and fully embraced these teachings, as follows:-

1. *Barrel*: Diogenes lived in a large ceramic jar / barrel / bathtub in the marketplace of Athens. He saw no need for the luxuries of a home, and considered his barrel sufficient for shelter.
2. *Alexander*: When Alexander the Great visited Diogenes, he asked if there was anything that he

could do for him. Diogenes replied, 'Yes, stand out of my sunlight.' He rejected the offer of assistance, showing his disdain for power and authority. The encounter left an impression on the young king. Alexander remarked, 'If I were not Alexander, I would be Diogenes.'

3. *Lamp*: Diogenes often carried around a lamp, claiming to be 'searching for an honest man.' This gesture was a satirical critique of the moral corruption he saw in society.
4. *Nudity*: Diogenes believed that clothing was unnecessary and cumbersome. He walked around naked or wearing a simple cloak, disregarding society's expectations of modesty.
5. *Public masturbation*: Diogenes was known to engage in public masturbation as a way to demonstrate his indifference to the opinions of others. He expressed his natural desires without shame.
6. *Alms*: Diogenes would beg for money while holding a statue, symbolising that most people worship material possessions. He aimed to provoke reflection on the true value of wealth.
7. *Eating*: Diogenes would eat his meals in the marketplace, regardless of who was watching. He considered food a basic necessity that should be consumed without concern for social etiquette.
8. *Scorn for politeness*: Diogenes disregarded niceties and mocked the conventions of polite behaviour. He would belch loudly, spit at people, and even urinate in public to challenge expectations of decorum.
9. *Dog-like*: Diogenes often likened himself to a dog, claiming to be 'the dog of the philosophers.' He lived

according to nature, as reflected in the behaviour of dogs.

10. *Death*: Diogenes died in his barrel at an old age. Legend has it that he instructed his friends to throw his body outside the city walls to be eaten by animals. This final act demonstrated his rejection of sacred customs even in death.

Influencer

Despite his unconventional lifestyle, Diogenes left a lasting legacy of uncompromising individuality. He had a significant influence on subsequent generations, such as: -

Stoics: The Stoical philosophers, including Zeno of Citium, embraced similar ideas of simplicity, self-control, and indifference to external circumstances.

Epicurus: Although Diogenes and Epicurus held different philosophical views, they shared a similar rejection of material wealth and a focus on simple contentment, and both emphasised living in accordance with nature.

Renaissance: Figures such as Michel de Montaigne and François Rabelais were inspired by Diogenes' questioning of authority.

Existentialists: Diogenes' radical individualism influenced modern thinkers in the 19th and 20th centuries, such as Friedrich Nietzsche and Jean-Paul Sartre, who were inspired by his authenticity and the constant questioning of inherited assumptions.

While Diogenes did not have a formal philosophical school, he left a legacy of amused admiration for his audacity, and the pursuit of a simple existence.

10th August 2023

76 Tekke

In every school in the United Kingdom, students are taught 'British Values'. These are: Democracy. The rule of law. Individual liberty. Mutual respect. And Tolerance - of those with different faiths and beliefs.

It is a foundational set of pillars. A legacy bequeathed to us by giants on whose shoulders we stand. These values find their roots in our Judeo-Christian heritage and our Graeco-Roman inheritance, alongside the clear-eyed rationalism and empiricism we absorbed from the Enlightenment.

Parthenon

Two hundred years ago, the Greek Resistance was fighting for independence, to free Greece from the rule of the Ottoman Turks.

In 1820, the Turks were using the Parthenon as a military barracks. They began using lead from the columns on the Parthenon, and melting it to make improvised bullets.

When the Greeks learnt of this sacrilegious desecration they were appalled. This magnificent monument had stood for 2,000 years, and symbolised Greece and everything it gave the world – democracy, mathematics, politics, theatre, philosophy, poetry, historiography, architecture, scientific method, medicine and medical ethics, the Olympic Games, rhetoric, oration, ethics, astronomy, and classical architecture.

These things are worth more than short-term, tactical disadvantage. So the Greeks sent the Turks a consignment of bullets, with the inscription: 'Here are your bullets, don't touch the pillars.'

Christopher Hitchens notes that 'no nobler action in time of war than this, worthy of the highest civilisation, can ever have been undertaken'.

Tekke

The *Hala Sultan Tekke* mosque is located on the banks of the Salt Lake in Larnaca, Cyprus. Its preservation, care and maintenance provides a stark contrast to the treatment of Christian heritage sites in the Turkish-occupied north of Cyprus.

Hala Sultan Tekke is the fourth most holy site in Islam, after Mecca, Medina and Jerusalem. It is believed to be the resting place of Umm Haram, a companion of the Prophet Muhammad.

The mosque and its surrounding area have been well preserved and maintained by the Republic of Cyprus. Restoration projects ensure its structural integrity and aesthetic preservation. The site is open to everyone, and remains a place of cultural significance.

I make a point of visiting it every time I'm in Cyprus. It's a tranquil spot.

Barbarism

In 1974, Turkey invaded Cyprus, on the pretext of defending Turkish Cypriots. Turkish Cypriots represented

18% of the Cyprus population and had lived in integrated villages – Greek and Turkish – for centuries. Since the invasion, Turkish troops have remained on the island, occupying the northern third.

Contrasts: 50 years on

In 2024, the Republic of Cyprus is a member of the European Union. Even without its top third of the island, it has a vibrant economy comprising financial services, shipping, agriculture, agrotourism, wind farms, tourism, real estate, construction, legal, accounting and consulting professional services, and manufacturing (including pharmaceuticals, food, beverages, cement).

This strong and legitimate track record contrasts strongly with the Turkish occupied north, which finances itself through prostitution, gambling, drugs, people trafficking, and handouts from Turkey.

There are approximately 600 Greek Orthodox churches and numerous cemeteries in the Turkish occupied north of Cyprus. Many churches have been desecrated, including acts of vandalism, looting, and graffiti. Religious artifacts have been stolen or destroyed.

When Boy George found out that a centuries-old Byzantine icon that he had bought at auction was stolen from a church in the north of Cyprus, he returned it to the Greek Orthodox church of *Saint Cosmas and Saint Damian* in Gospel Oak, north London.

Several churches have been converted into stables or warehouses, with no regard for their historical and cultural significance. Many sites have been left to decay, with no maintenance or preservation efforts.

We've been here before, and there is only one winner – civilisation always triumphs over barbarism.

We have the Parthenon. We have Cyprus.

26th July 2024

77 Resistance

Red resistance

Whilst the word 'communist' is often a derogatory term, there have been moments in history when its proponents have served humanity well. Greece demonstrated a dignified example of this.

The Communist Party of Greece (KKE) played a critical role in resisting the Greek military junta, a fascist regime that ruled Greece from 1967 to 1974. In Greece, the KKE and other left-wing groups became symbols of resistance and bravery, fighting against a dictatorship that sought to crush democratic freedoms and impose authoritarian rule.

Power – The 1967 coup

The military junta, also known as the Regime of the Colonels, came to power through a coup d'état on April 21st, 1967. The coup was carried out by a group of right-wing army officers who feared that the left-wing political forces, particularly the United Democratic Left (EDA) and the KKE, would win in the upcoming elections. The junta justified its actions by claiming it was saving Greece from a communist takeover, a fear that was commonplace and deeply rooted in the Cold War era.

The junta imposed many anti-democratic measures: it suspended the constitution, dissolved parliament, and imposed strict censorship, widespread arrests, and torture, and sent political opponents into exile. The regime sought to eliminate all forms of dissent and used violence and intimidation to maintain control.

The Left's resistance

The KKE, despite being banned and heavily persecuted, played a central role in organising and inspiring resistance against the junta. Underground networks were formed to distribute anti-junta propaganda, organise strikes, and mobilise protests. The KKE's resilience in the face of severe repression made it a focal point of the broader resistance movement.

The most famous act of resistance was the Athens Polytechnic uprising in November 1973. Students occupied the Athens Polytechnic University, demanding the end of the dictatorship and the restoration of democracy. The junta responded with brutal force, sending in tanks to crush the rebellion, resulting in numerous deaths and injuries.

Fall

The regime's downfall was precipitated by its involvement in the Cyprus crisis. In July 1974, the junta supported a coup in Cyprus to overthrow President Makarios and unite the island with Greece, provoking a Turkish invasion. The resulting conflict and the catastrophic consequences for Greece and Cyprus led to a collapse of the junta's authority.

Faced with the Cyprus disaster and massive popular discontent, the military junta stepped down, and Greece transitioned back to democracy in July 1974. Former Prime

Minister Konstantinos Karamanlis was invited back from exile to lead the new government.

Acts

Alexandros Panagoulis was a key figure in the anti-junta resistance. Panagoulis attempted to assassinate junta leader Georgios Papadopoulos in 1968. Though the attempt failed, his subsequent capture, trial, and torture made him a symbol of resistance. Despite enduring horrific torture, he remained defiant, refusing to betray his comrades. After the fall of the junta, Panagoulis was elected to the Greek parliament but died under mysterious circumstances in 1976.

Although executed in 1952, Nikos Beloyannis remains a symbol of resistance in Greece. Known as 'The Man with the Carnation', he fought against the Axis occupation during World War II and later against the monarchists and fascists in the Greek Civil War. His trial and execution by the post-war government were widely seen as a miscarriage of justice, and he became a national martyr.

In Greece, during the junta years, 'communist' was not a political label but a symbol of resistance against tyranny and oppression. The KKE and other leftist organisations demonstrated immense courage in the face of brutal repression, fighting for human rights during one of the darkest periods in the nation's history.

19th August 2024

XIV – Language

Kurtz: *Are my methods unsound?*

Willard: *I don't see, any method, at all, sir.*

– *Apocalypse Now*

78 Sandinistas

Reading in Nicaragua: 1979 – 1990

Nicaragua is the largest country in Central America. Its multi-ethnic population of six million includes people of indigenous, European and African heritage. The main language is Spanish. Indigenous tribes on the *Mosquito Coast* speak their own languages and English.

'Yes, I can'

During their initial rule from 1979 to 1990, the Sandinista government, led by the political party *Frente Sandinista de Liberación Nacional (FSLN)*, implemented an extensive literacy programme in Nicaragua. The educational campaign, the '*National Literacy Crusade*', was launched in 1980 with the goal of eradicating illiteracy, running at 50%, in the country.

This was a grassroots programme, involving thousands of volunteers, known as '*brigadistas*', who were trained to teach basic reading and writing skills. These *brigadistas* primarily consisted of young people, teachers, and students who travelled to rural areas and impoverished neighbourhoods, where illiteracy rates were highest. They lived among the local communities, learning their dialects and cultural nuances, which helped establish trust and effective communication.

The campaign used a variety of innovative teaching methods. The *'Yo, sí puedo' (Yes, I Can)* method developed by Cuba, which employed audio-visual materials, such as television and radio broadcasts, significantly enhanced the learning experience. This approach allowed adults to learn at their own pace and offered flexibility with work and family responsibilities.

Thousands of individuals, who were previously excluded from economic, social, and political opportunities due to their illiteracy, gained access to basic education. The programme also fostered a sense of community and solidarity, as Nicaraguans from different backgrounds came together to support the national effort.

The programme won an award from UNESCO, the United Nations Educational and Cultural Organisation.

No saints

While the literacy programme was undoubtedly a success, other aspects of the Sandinista government faced criticism.

The Sandinistas implemented measures that limited freedom of speech, curtailed press freedom, and suppressed opposition parties. These actions undermined democratic principles and led to the polarisation of Nicaraguan society.

Additionally, the government's economic policies, including the implementation of a centrally planned economy and the nationalisation of industries, resulted in significant economic instability and declining living standards. The country faced a severe economic crisis, characterised by hyper-inflation, shortages of basic goods, and high levels of unemployment.

While the literacy programme achieved remarkable success in reducing illiteracy and empowering marginalised communities, the restrictions on civil liberties, economic instability, and regional military involvement, tarnished the Sandinistas.

U.S.A.

The role of the United States in undermining the Sandinista government was significant and had a substantial impact on their downfall in 1990. The Reagan administration pursued a policy of active intervention in Nicaragua, aiming to counter the Sandinistas' socialist agenda.

The US imposed economic sanctions and embargos, severely impacting Nicaragua's economy. These measures included trade restrictions, the freezing of Nicaraguan assets in the United States, and the denial of loans from financial institutions. The economic sanctions led to a decline in foreign investment, hindered economic development, and contributed to high levels of unemployment and poverty in the country.

Outcomes

The US blockers notwithstanding, results of the literacy campaign were something to be proud of. Illiteracy decreased from an estimated 50% to just 13% within a year. Also, the interaction between urban and rural populations had a deep impact on young people and gave them new insights into the realities of their country.

A longitudinal study (repeated observations over very long periods) indicated that women who had become literate as adults in 1980 went on to have healthier children (Daniel, P., 2002).

Many of the *brigadistas,* energised by their experiences on the literacy programme decided to go into teaching as a career.

19th October 2023

79 Money

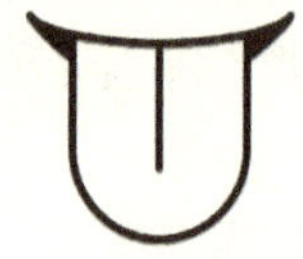

Money before language

Money emerged before language in human history. Early human societies sought increasingly efficient methods of trade and cooperation.

Our early ancestors lived in small, nomadic groups where survival depended heavily on hunting. In such small communities, the need for complex language was limited. Instead, rudimentary forms of communication, consisting of gestures, vocalisation, and simple symbols, was enough for basic survival.

Trade and exchange were essential for accessing resources that were not locally available. Early humans engaged in barter systems, exchanging goods directly. However, barter systems can be inefficient and cumbersome, especially when attempting to exchange goods with different perceived values. Imagine trying to trade a cow for wheat without a shared agreement of value.

Shells and furs

This inefficiency led to the development of primitive forms of money. Objects with value, such as seashells, animal pelts, or agricultural produce, were used as proto-money. These objects had value in themselves, were easy to carry, and served as a medium of exchange within a community. They predated the need for a complex language system because their value was universally understood within the group, and between groups.

These early forms of money were symbolic and required little verbal communication. They conveyed value through physical presence, avoiding the need for elaborate language to express worth or to negotiate exchanges. A person holding a pouch of earth minerals or a bundle of furs could communicate value effectively without uttering a single word.

As human societies expanded, so did the complexity of their economic activities. Proto-money evolved into standardised forms like tokens or small metal objects, further reducing the reliance on language in economic transactions. The acceptance of these standard forms of money within a society required basic agreement and trust rather than the extensive communication language necessary for negotiations.

Cities

The establishment of the first cities in Mesopotamia (c. 3000 BCE) provided the infrastructure for the next simplest form of money of account - asset-backed credit. Farmers would deposit their grain in the temple which recorded the deposit on clay tablets and gave the farmer a receipt in the form of a clay token which they could then use to pay fees or debts to the temple. Since most of the deposits in the temple were of the main staple, barley, a fixed quantity of barley came to be used as a unit of account.

Language, on the other hand, emerged as a tool for sharing knowledge, stories, and beliefs within larger communities. Its development was closely tied to the evolution of settled agriculture and the need to organise collective activities like farming, construction, and defence. With the rise of agriculture, the ability to communicate became crucial, as larger groups needed to coordinate activities and allocate resources.

While language flourished within communities, the role of money expanded beyond the confines of small groups. As trade networks grew and societies became more interconnected, standardised money helped to conduct economic interactions among strangers. Money's universal common acceptance allowed individuals from different backgrounds to engage in trade and cooperation without a common language.

This universality of money has persisted throughout history, transcending linguistic, cultural, and geographical boundaries.

Language is a dynamic and evolving construct, subject to variations. Dialects, accents, and idioms abound within a single language, making effective communication a challenge in diverse settings. Money, however, provides a stable and universally understood medium for trade, bypassing linguistic barriers.

Money is not just a medium of exchange but also a store of value and a unit of account. These functions of money require precision and stability, which are best achieved through standardised symbols or tokens.

11th January 2024

80 Monkey

Monkey magic

'Nobody ever saw a dog exchange of one bone for another with another dog. Nobody ever saw them signify I am willing to give this for that.'

- Adam Smith, founder of classical economics, 1776

When Keith Chen was Associate Professor of Economics at *Yale University,* he was inspired by this quote from Adam Smith to ask, 'What would happen if I could teach monkeys to use money?'

Seven capuchin monkeys (known as 'organ grinder' monkeys) were set up in a lab at the *Yale-New Haven Hospital.* In the tradition of monkey labs everywhere, the monkeys were given names – in this case, from characters in James Bond films. There were four females and three males. The alpha male was named Felix, after the CIA agent Felix Leiter.

The monkeys lived together in a large, open cage. For currency, Chen used a one-inch silver disc with a hole in the middle.

First step: teach the monkeys that the coins had value.

If you give a monkey a coin, they will sniff it and, after determining they can't eat it or have sex with it, they'll throw it away.

The researchers gave a monkey a coin and then showed a treat. Whenever the monkey gave the coin back to the researcher, it got the treat. It took many months, but the monkeys eventually learned that the coins could buy the treats.

Individual monkeys had preferences for different treats. A monkey would be presented with twelve coins on a tray - their budget - and then be offered jelly cubes by one researcher and apple slices by another. The monkey would hand over his coins to whichever researcher held the food he preferred.

Price shocks were introduced into this economy. Felix was accustomed to getting three cubes of jelly for one coin. How would he respond if one coin suddenly bought just two cubes?

Felix and the others responded rationally. When the price of a given food rose, the monkeys bought less of it, and when the price fell, they bought more. The basic law of economics - the demand curve slopes downward - held for monkeys as well as humans.

Then the strangest thing happened in the lab

One day, Felix did not use his coins to buy food. Instead, he threw the coins into the communal cage and dashed in after them.

There was chaos in the cage, with twelve coins on the floor and seven monkeys going after them. When the researchers tried to get the coins, the monkeys wouldn't give them up.

After all, they'd learned that the coins had value. So the humans began bribing the monkeys with treats.

Then Chen saw something remarkable happen.

One monkey, rather than handing his coin over to the humans for a grape or a slice of apple, instead approached a second monkey and gave it to her. Chen had done earlier research that showed monkeys could be altruistic. Had he just witnessed an act of monkey altruism?

After a few seconds of grooming, the two monkeys were having sex.

It wasn't altruism at all, but rather the first instance of monkey prostitution in the recorded history of science.

And to prove how thoroughly the monkeys had assimilated the concept of money, as soon as the sex was over, the female monkey who'd received the coin promptly brought it over to Chen to purchase some grapes.

Alas, full monkey capitalism never came to pass. The lab authorities intervened, fearing that introducing money to the monkeys would irreparably damage their social structure.

They were probably right.

29th September 2024

81 Names

James with the names

'Tis but thy name that is my enemy.
What's in a name? That which we call a rose
By any other name would smell as sweet.'
- Romeo and Juliet, II, 2

Names have meaning.

They tell a story of work, or place or ancestry, or all of these things at once.

In England, the surnames Cooper, Tanner, Miller, Shepherd, Fisher, Archer all derive from the occupation of their ancestor.

You know that a Ramsbottom, a Haythornthwaite and a Kershaw come from Yorkshire.

A Rawlinson, a Whittaker and a Pilkington, are from Lancashire.

A Lumsden, a Pemberton and a Milburn, from the North East of England.

Northern Italian: Rossi, Bianchi, Conti.

Southern Italian: Romano, Marino, Mancini.

Northern French: Moreau, Dubois, Lambert.

Southern French: Arnaud, Giraud, Blanc.

Greek surnames similarly hold significance.

Prefixes

Archi: meaning 'superior' or 'boss'.

Chondro: meaning 'fat'.

Gero: 'old' or 'wise'.

Hadji: the Arabic for one who has made the Hadj or pilgrimage, used in the case of Christians for a voyage to Jerusalem, for example 'Hatzipanagis'.

Kara: the Turkish word for 'black'.

Konto: meaning 'short'.

Makro: meaning 'tall' or 'long'.

Mastro: 'artisan' or 'workman' or 'expert crafstman'.

Palaio: 'old' or 'wise'.

Papa: indicating descent from a *papas,* a priest. So Papakostas is the 'son of Kostas, the priest'.

Suffixes

-akis (-άκης): associated primarily with Crete and the Aegean Islands, it is a diminutive (a form of words that convey a smaller size or a sense of endearment or affection) – such as Giorgos becoming Giorgakis for the 'young Giorgos'. Examples are: 'Mitsotakis', 'Theodorakis' and 'Doukakis'. This suffix was also very common for Cretan Turks up until they were officially changed with the Surname Law.

-akos (-άκος): mainly from Laconia, particularly among Maniots from the Laconian part of the Mani peninsula.

-oulis (-ούλης): mainly from Thessalia, it is a diminutive for place names in the region such as Giannouli and Damasouli.

-as (-άς): from Macedonia and the Epirus. Examples are: 'Melas', 'Dimas', 'Zorbas', 'Moustakas' and 'Zappas'.

-atos (-άτος): (from Cephalonia), originally Venetian.

-eas (-εας): mainly among Maniots from the Messenian part of the Mani peninsula.

-elis (-έλης) and -ilis (-ιλής): from the Turkish suffixes for agent, possession and origin, common in western Asia Minor, Mytiline, Lemnos and Imbros.

-allis (-άλλης) and -ellis (-έλλης): both found especially in the Dodecanese, mainly Rhodes.

-idis or -ides and -iadis or iades (-ίδης/-ιάδης): meaning 'son of' or 'descendant of'.

The suffix -idis (often transliterated as -ides in English and French) is the oldest in use. Zeus, for example, was also referred to as Cronides ('son of Cronus'). -idis was the most common suffix in Byzantium, Bithynia and Thrace, being also used by Pontic Greeks and Caucasus Greeks in the Pontic Alps, northeast Anatolia, Georgia, the former Kars Oblast, and sometimes in Epirus, Corfu and some Aegean islands.

-lis (-λής). Turkish suffix for 'of' a place, like the suffixes -tis and -otis.

-opoulos (-όπουλος): meaning 'descendant of', originated from the Peloponnese but has become very widespread. It can also indicate ethnic origin, such as Frangopoulos (Φραγκόπουλος) meaning 'son of a Frank', Persopoulos (Περσόπουλος) meaning 'son of a Persian', Servopoulos (Σερβόπουλος) meaning 'son of a Serb' and Voulgaropoulos (Βουλγαρόπουλος) meaning 'son of a Bulgarian'.

-oglou (-όγλου): from the Turkish -oğlu meaning 'son of', seen in families from Asia Minor.

-ou (-ου): a genitive mainly from Cyprus.

-tis, -otis (-της, -ώτης): meaning 'of' a place. Examples are 'Politis' meaning from the city, and 'Chiotis' from Chios.

-tzis, -tsis (-τζής, -τσής) and feminine (-τζή, -τσή): Turkish suffix to signify a profession, like the English -er in Baker or Butcher.

15th August 2024

82 Words

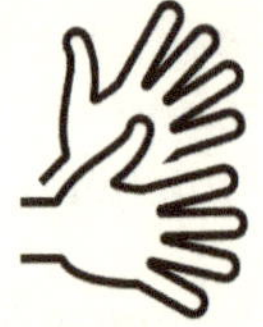

Words that work: Rules for clear English from two masters

In his well-known and celebrated essay *Politics and the English Language* (1946), George Orwell attacks the decline of clear writing, which he thought was directly linked to political manipulation.

He condemns clichés and jargon that obscure meaning.

Orwell promotes simple, direct prose, so that language can convey truth and clarity, and that good writing can reflect precise thought.

So he developed some rules, which are themselves as refreshing as cold, running water. And like pretty much everything that Orwell wrote, these rules stand the test of time.

1. Never use a metaphor, simile, or other figure of speech which you are used to seeing in print.
2. Never use a long word where a short one will do.
3. If it is possible to cut a word out, always cut it out.
4. Never use the passive where you can use the active.

5. Never use a foreign phrase, a scientific word, or a jargon word if you can think of an everyday English equivalent.
6. Break any of these rules sooner than say anything outright barbarous.

Orwell takes aim at '*pretentious words* ... that are used to dress up simple statements and give an air of scientific impartiality to biased judgments ... Adjectives like *epoch-making, epic, historic, unforgettable, triumphant, age-old, inevitable, inexorable, veritable,* are used to dignify sordid international politics. Expressions such as *cul de sac, ancien régime, status quo,* are used to give an air of culture and elegance. There is no real need for these words.'

In *Tribune* magazine, he says, 'Why say cul-de-sac when you mean blind alley? For two hundred years we got on well enough with 'coffee house', do we really need the word café?'

Impact

In his highly enjoyable book, '*Words that Work*' (2006), Dr Frank Luntz, the veteran pollster and focus group guru, sets out the most impactful words, and why they work.

Luntz argues that effective communication hinges on understanding the audience and tailoring language to resonate with their values, emotions, and beliefs.

He advocated using vocabulary that's crafted to produce the desired effect, such as 'death tax' instead of 'estate tax', and 'climate change' instead of 'global warming'. He also advised describing Palestinian negotiating points as 'demands', because Americans dislike people who make *demands*.

Here are some of his most effective words *that work*.

'Imagine': engages the audience's creativity, and gets them to visualise *something better*.

'Hassle free': this wording invokes a sense of urgency and immediacy. It suggests prompt action, appealing to us because we value time.

'Lifestyle': is incredibly powerful because it is self-defined as well as aspirational.

'You': personalises the message, making it more direct and relevant to the listener.

'Results, Revitalise, Renew': focuses on outcomes and benefits. We all care about those.

'Innovation': invokes curiosity and the excitement in finding something new and valuable.

'Certified, Proven': offers assurance and builds trust in the reliability of a product or service, by implying evidence and consistent success.

These words work because they tap into our human need for security, our value of time, and the appeal of novelty and personal relevance.

Politics

I recently said the phrase 'homeless person', when chatting to my son. He said, 'You mean 'unhoused person' '.

That might be the currently acceptable phrase, but I'm not sure it's *clearer*. It just sounds like the phrase points the finger at someone else; the *someone else* who should be doing the housing. It's loaded with the insistence that it isn't the homeless person's fault. That may be true, but it's a lot to load into a phrase.

Being the clear and expert communicator that he is, Dr Luntz has advised several governments and political parties on their messaging and communications. He was especially entertaining on an episode of *Times Radio*'s '*How To Win An Election*' in June 2024, talking about both of the upcoming UK and US elections.

He scorned the Democrats' blinkered, protracted and erroneous insistence on Joe Biden's suitability as a candidate.

Frank's punchlines came thick and fast: 'Joe Biden is so old it takes him an hour and a half to watch the show '*60 Minutes*' ... He's so old his favourite painting is the *Last Supper;* he's actually in the painting ... He calls himself a constitutionalist, he was in the room when they wrote the document ... The only time Joe Biden doesn't have to pee, is when he's peeing.'

In a 2007 interview on the *NPR* programme *Fresh Air*, Luntz argued that the term '*Orwellian*' could be considered in a positive sense. He explained, 'if one reads George Orwell's essay *Politics and the English Language*, to be 'Orwellian' is to speak with absolute clarity, to be succinct, to explain what the event is, to talk about what triggers something happening… and to do so without any pejorative meaning whatsoever.'

Luntz suggested that Orwell would not have approved of many of the uses of the term, given that his essay derides the use of cliché and dying metaphors.

5th January 2025

83 Alexander

The names of Alexander

Alexander the Great's name left a profound mark on the regions he conquered, influencing local languages and cultures. In many parts of Asia and the Indian subcontinent, his name was adopted, adapted, and transformed over time. There are some notable derivations.

Sikandar (ردنکس)

Region: Persian-speaking regions, South Asia (India, Pakistan, Afghanistan).

Origins: Derived from the Greek *Alexandros* via its Old Persian adaptation, *Eskandar*.

Impact: Sikandar became synonymous with a great conqueror or hero. In Indian history and literature, the name was sometimes used to signify an ideal warrior or a formidable leader. For example, Emperor Akbar of the Mughal Empire was often compared to 'Sikandar-e-Asam' (Alexander the Great).

Iskandar (ردنكسإ)

Region: Arabic-speaking regions, Indonesia, and Malaysia.

Origins: This is the Arabic adaptation of Alexander's name, derived from the Persian *Eskandar*.

Cultural Impact: The name Iskandar appears in Islamic and Middle Eastern traditions, often connected to legends like *Dhu al-Qarnayn*, a figure in the Quran sometimes identified with Alexander. In Southeast Asia, the name Iskandar remains a common given name.

Eskandar (ردنکسا)

Region: Iran and surrounding Persian-influenced regions.

Origins: A direct Persian adaptation of *Alexandros*.

Impact: Alexander is often romanticised in Persian literature, particularly in Ferdowsi's *Shahnameh*, where he is portrayed as a wise and just ruler.

Al-Iskandariyya (ةيردنكسإلا)

Region: Egypt and the Arab world.

Origins: The Arabic name for the city of Alexandria, founded by Alexander in 331 BCE.

Cultural Impact: Alexandria became a major cultural and intellectual hub in the ancient world, its name immortalised in various languages.

Sekandar

Region: Pashto-speaking regions of Afghanistan and Pakistan.

Origins: A localised variant of *Sikandar* used in Pashto literature and folk tales.

Lekander / Aleksandar

Region: Central Asia, particularly in areas influenced by Turkic and Persian cultures.

Origins: Variations influenced by both Greek and local linguistic patterns.

Kandar or Khandar

Region: South Asia (particularly in folk tales).

Origins: Abbreviated or altered versions of *Sikandar*, found in oral traditions and stories.

Folklore

In South Asia and the Middle East, Alexander (as Sikandar/Iskandar) is a recurring figure, and is often depicted as a wise and adventurous ruler, sometimes intertwined with mythical figures. For instance, in Persian lore, Alexander's conquests are romanticised, and he is portrayed as a seeker of wisdom.

Many cities named after Alexander still bear variations of his name, such as Alexandria in Egypt, and Kandahar in Afghanistan.

The name Sikandar or Iskandar became a metaphor for supreme leadership and heroism in many literary traditions, including Urdu and Hindi poetry.

From *Sikandar* to *Iskandar*, Alexander's name has been adapted into numerous languages and traditions across Asia, each reflecting his enduring influence as a conqueror and a cultural icon. These adaptations are a testament to the profound legacy of his campaigns, which not only spread Greek learning and culture, but also integrated and inspired the local civilisations he encountered.

4th January 2025

XV - Sport

'Five days shalt thou labour, as the Bible says.
The seventh day is the Lord thy God's.
The sixth day is for football.'
- Anthony Burgess

84 Fans

A Fan's Life: Masculinity, hubris and an almost fanatical devotion to hope

All devoted football fans know that feeling when the 'red mist' descends on seeing their team concede a crucial goal or lose an important match. Using MRI (*Magnetic Resonance Imaging*) scans, scientists have now discovered what is happening in their brains.

In the most avid supporters, the region in the brain governing 'cognitive control' experiences a shutdown when their team is losing, leaving them more likely to 'fall into disruptive or violent behaviour', a study has found.

In less excitable fans, seeing their team losing provokes a less aggressive and more 'introspective' response, the researchers from Chile discovered.

When dedicated fans see their team score or win, the reward centres of their brain light up, 'inducing pleasure sensations'.

Dr Francisco Zamorano, from San Sebastián University in Santiago, Chile, took two sets of fans – 22 who supported *Colo-Colo* and 21 who supported *Universidad de Chile*, two fierce rivals in Chilean football.

The fans underwent psychological evaluations to place them on a 'football supporters' fanaticism scale'. They were then hooked up to a functional magnetic resonance imaging (*fMRI*) system to analyse blood flow through their brains while they were shown a compilation of footage from football matches. This featured their team scoring and conceding goals and also showed their main rivals scoring and conceding.

'When their team wins, the reward system in the brain is activated,' Dr Zamorano said. 'When they lose, the mentalisation network can be activated, taking the fan to an introspective state. This may mitigate some of the pain of the loss.'

The findings may help in situations outside sport, the researchers hope, where tribalism can cause 'societal discord'.

In most fans, seeing their team lose or their rivals win had a more serious impact. 'We also observed inhibition of the brain hub that connects the limbic system with frontal cortices, hampering the mechanism that regulates cognitive control and increasing the probability to fall into disruptive or anti-social behaviour.'

In calmer fans, this 'mentalising network' allows the brain to process and understand emotional states in the self and in others, helping to maintain a sense of calm that can elude more enthusiastic supporters.

Dr Zamorano said that his findings, which he presented to the *Radiological Society of North America*, could be applied outside sport, in other social settings where people show tribal loyalty so fierce that it can lead to 'unreasoned beliefs and societal discord'.

The research said: 'Fanaticism is extreme or excessive devotion or enthusiasm towards a particular cause, belief or opinion. It often involves blind and unquestioning loyalty to a particular ideology or leader and a refusal to consider other perspectives or opinions.

'Fanaticism can lead to intolerance and aggression toward those who do not share the same beliefs. In this sense, the study proposes a new model for studying complex behaviours like fanaticism.'

Zamorano said that football supporters were a perfect group in which to analyse these effects because football is generally less controversial than politics or religion. 'Sports fandom presents a unique opportunity to analyse how intense devotion affects neural activity in a less contentious context, by highlighting the role of negative emotions, the related inhibitory control mechanisms and possible adaptative strategies,' he said.

'Understanding the psychology of group identification and competition can shed light on decision-making processes and social dynamics, leading to a fuller comprehension of how societies operate.'

25th January 2024

85 1:59

INEOS doesn't do PowerPoints, it does actions

Can the marathon be run in under 2 hours?

The *INEOS 1:59 Project* was an ambitious athletic endeavour aimed at achieving the seemingly impossible.

Organised by British chemical company INEOS with Kenyan marathon runner Eliud Kipchoge, the event took place on October 12th, 2019, in Vienna, Austria.

Kipchoge completed the marathon distance (42 kilometres / 26 miles) in **1 hour, 59 minutes, and 40 seconds**, becoming the first person in history to break the two-hour barrier.

Although the run was not eligible for official world record status - due to the use of supporting runners who rotated as pace-makers, a flat course, and other controlled conditions - it was nevertheless celebrated as a monumental human achievement.

The project demonstrated the extraordinary limits of human endurance and was a showcase of meticulous planning, technological innovation, and Kipchoge's remarkable athleticism. Over the marathon's 42km, his almost super-human ability enabled him to achieve a 2 minute and 50 second time for each 1km, on average.

The project was a highly coordinated and multidisciplinary effort that required collaboration across various fields, bringing together experts from different domains to create the perfect conditions.

Key areas of collaboration

1. *Sports analytics*

Formula 1 expertise: Engineers and analysts from the INEOS-backed *Mercedes-AMG Petronas* Formula 1 Team played a crucial role in analysing Kipchoge's running form, optimising pacing strategies, and refining the positioning of pacemakers. Their experience in high-performance motorsport analytics fine-tuned every aspect of Kipchoge's run to maximise efficiency and speed.

2. *Weather planning*

Sailing team insights: The *INEOS Team UK*, which competes in the *America's Cup* sailing race, provided weather forecasting expertise. The team's knowledge of wind patterns, humidity, and temperature control selected the ideal day and time for the marathon in Vienna, ensuring that Kipchoge ran in optimal conditions.

3. *Course selection and design*

Precision course planning: The course in Vienna was chosen for its flatness, minimal turns, and consistent surface, reducing any unnecessary strain on Kipchoge. The Prater Park in Vienna offered a straight, 9.6 km loop with gentle curves, minimising energy loss and maintaining

Kipchoge's rhythm. INEOS even had to re-surface some tarmac on a roundabout along the route, to make it flatter.

4. *Pacing strategy*

Rotating pacemakers: A team of 41 world-class runners took turns running in a V-formation around Kipchoge, helping him maintain a consistent pace. This required precise timing and coordination, ensuring that each pacemaker group integrated seamlessly.

5. *Footwear*

Nike's Vaporfly shoes: *Nike* designed a customised version of their *Vaporfly* running shoes for Kipchoge, incorporating carbon fibre plates and advanced foam to enhance energy return and reduce fatigue over the marathon distance.

6. *Nutrition and hydration*

Custom nutritional plan: Kipchoge's nutrition and hydration were meticulously planned, with energy gels and drinks delivered to him by a cyclist at precisely calculated intervals. This ensured he maintained peak energy levels without the risk of gastrointestinal issues or dehydration.

7. *Mental preparation*

Mindset coaching: Beyond the physical and technical aspects, Kipchoge's mental preparation was a critical focus. Psychologists and coaches worked with him to maintain focus, motivation, and confidence - all crucial elements for enduring such a high-pressure, historic challenge.

The scale of the effort

There was significant logistical coordination in organising the event in Vienna, liaising with the city's officials, ensuring the safety and timing of the event, and managing a global media presence.

Currently, the *official* men's marathon world record is 2:00:35, set by Kelvin Kiptum of Kenya in 2023, at the Chicago Marathon. This time surpassed the previous record of 2:01:09, held by Eliud Kipchoge, set at the Berlin Marathon in 2022.

15th September 2024

XVI – Community

Neighbour: *Can you keep your voices down, please?*
I've husband on nights.

Auntie Annie: *Frig off! And wash your bastad curtains, you dirty cow!*

– *East is East (1999)*

86 Philosemitism

Jewishness and the English language

Nobel Prizes have been awarded to over 900 individuals, of whom 22% were Jews. A hugely disproportionate achievement, as the Jewish people account for only 0.2% of the world's population.

The word *antisemitism* was coined in the 1870s by a German journalist called Wilhelm Marr. His intention was 'to get people to stop hating the Jews for religious reasons, and start hating them for cultural and racial reasons' (Martin Amis).

Voltaire said that Judaism was to be objected to, not just in itself as a religion, but on the even stronger grounds that Judaism has the terrible tendency to lead to Christianity.

It has never gone away. A certain kind of *bien pensant* in England is never more gorgeously at his ease, never more exquisitely complacent, than when attacking Israel, and trying to de-legitimise it.

Socialist internationalism. Nuclear physics. Psychotherapy. Modernist fiction. The law. Classical music. Comedy. From the early 19th century to the modern day, the Jewish people have been major contributors to all these fields.

In his later life, aged 40, writer Christopher Hitchens discovered that he was in fact Jewish. He was asked whether he felt unease in England or America. He said 'I don't ever expect or actually want to feel *at ease*. I don't think it's in the fate or nature of the Jewish people to feel at ease, or at home. We are doomed to exile and diaspora. I don't want to become complacent. Insecure, unstable, that's fine. I don't want a quiet life. Also don't expect one.'

There's a wonderful expression in the diaries of Victor Klemperer, a German Jew during the 1930s, when the net tightened around him and his friends. Klemperer says that 'we are a seismic people. We can always see what's coming, we register the tremors ahead of everyone else.'

What draws us, magnetically to the Jewish tradition, is the tremendous contribution of Marx and Freud, of Einstein and Kafka, of Billy Wilder and Woody Allen.

When Henry James started to try and define the idea of an English literature written by Americans in the American scene, the thing that most horrified him, when he returned to the New York that he thought belonged to him, was the prevalence of *Yiddishkeit* – 'The murder of the English language,' said James, 'in the torture rooms of the Jewish coffee houses.'

He couldn't believe that the pure well of English had been so defiled by these 'aliens of Israel', as he called them. And for a very long time this became a feeling and even policy in American academic life. The literary critic Lionel Trilling (1905 – 1975), was refused tenure as a professor at Columbia University, on the grounds that 'as a Marxist, a Freudian and a Jew' (and they might as well just have come right out with it), he wouldn't be able to understand the specially sensitive register of English literature, let alone teach it to others.

The Yiddish street lingo, was thus fused with English, and was ennobled by Isaac Bashevis Singer. And decades later, it was brought into the mainstream by Saul Bellow, Norman Mailer, Philip Roth and Joseph Heller. Bellow translated T.S Eliot's *The Love Song of J. Alfred Prufrock* into Yiddish. It was latent revenge on H. James.

Jesus and Mohamed have one thing in common. They first introduced themselves to the local Jewish population, saying that they were going to vindicate their prophecies. And after the Jews had had a square look at both of them, they said, 'No. Not for us. We will still wait.'

It seems this isn't going to be forgiven.

28th October 2023

87 Merry

The 'Merry' cemetery

'A dreaded sunny day,
So I'll meet you at the cemetery gates,
Keats and Yeats are on your side,
But you lose, because Wilde is on mine.'
- Morrissey/Marr

'In the midst of life, we are in death', says the *Book of Common Prayer* (1662).

When someone dies, their memory generally enters an idealised realm in the minds of those who loved them. Their flaws are forgiven and forgotten, and their offences overlooked. For the faithful, they pass among the spirits of the righteous into a place of light, green pasture, and refreshment.

The way in which they passed away often goes unspoken.

Not so in the town of Sapanta, Romania. In the *'Merry Cemetery'*, over 800 wooden crosses tell the life stories, intimate details, and final moments of the townsfolk - displayed in bright, colourful pictures and annotated with jokes and stories of the departed.

Illustrated crosses depict soldiers being beheaded and a townsperson being hit by a truck. The epigraphs reveal a surprising level of truth. One states: '*Underneath this heavy cross lies my mother in law. Try not to wake her up. If she comes back home. She'll bite my head off.*'

Stan Ioan Pătraş was born in Sapanta in 1908, and started carving crosses for the cemetery at the age of 14. By 1935, Pătraş had begun carving ironic inscriptions in the local dialect about the deceased, as well as painting the crosses with their image, often including the way in which they died.

He developed a symbolism in his carvings. Green represented life, yellow represented fertility, red for passion, black for death. The colours were painted on a deep blue, known as Sapanta blue, which represented hope, freedom, and the sky. Other symbolism – white doves for the soul, a blackbird to represent a tragic or suspicious death – made their way onto the crosses, as did a dark sense of humour.

One carving reads, '*Ioan Toaderu loved horses. One more thing he loved very much. To sit at a table in a bar. Next to someone else's wife.*'

Pătraş died in 1977, having carved his own cross and left his house and work to his most talented apprentice, Dumitru Pop, who continued the craft. The grave slabs are made of oak. Pop cuts the trees down himself.

Despite the dark comedy, no-one has ever complained. 'It's the real life of a person. If he likes to drink, you say that; if he likes to work, you say that. The families want the true life of the person to be represented on the cross.'

Pop says that the work can get repetitive. 'Their lives were the same, but they want their epitaphs to be different.' A book called '*The Crosses of Sapanta*' lists the captions in the cemetery.

Even the Romanian Communists embraced the Merry Cemetery. The grave of Communist official Ioan Holdis shows a hammer and sickle and a Bible. The inscription says: *'As long as I lived, I loved the Party. And all my life I tried to help the people.'*

Ethnologists say Sapanta's laughing cemetery is likely a reflection of attitudes that come from the time of the Dacians, early inhabitants of Romania, and have been passed down in folklore ever since. The historian Herodotus said the Dacians were fearless in battle and went laughing to their graves because they believed they were going to meet Zalmoxis, their supreme god.

The Reverend Grigore Lutai, Sapanta's Orthodox priest, agrees. 'The people here don't react to death as though it were a tragedy,' he said. 'Death is just a passage to another life.'

14th March 2024

88 Kitchen

Hidden gems: World Central Kitchen

Food is life – especially in a crisis.

A thoughtful, freshly-prepared meal is one less thing someone has to worry about in the wake of a disaster. It is a reminder that you are not alone, someone is thinking about you, and someone cares. Food has the power to be the nourishment and hope we need to pick ourselves back up in the darkest times.

In 2010, expert Chef José Andrés, was ready to use his culinary knowledge and talent to help. He headed to Haiti following a devastating earthquake. Cooking alongside displaced families in a camp, he was guided on the proper way to cook black beans the way Haitians like to eat them: mashed and sieved into a creamy sauce.

It was about feeding people in need—but it was also about listening, learning, and cooking side by side with the people impacted by the crisis.

José, and his wife Patricia, founded *World Central Kitchen (WCK),* a not-for-profit, non-governmental organisation that provides local food relief.

It gets on the ground quickly, and sets up local supply chains using domestic logistics. It sources native ingredients, and cooks the recipes that people in crisis recognise, instead of alien, generic, vacuum-packed, powdered food.

WCK has contributed to the provision of meals in Australia, the Bahamas, the Dominican Republic, Egypt, Israel, Lebanon, Puerto Rico, Ukraine, the United States, Turkey, Syria, and Palestine. It has also operated culinary training programmes in Cambodia, the Dominican Republic, Nicaragua, Zambia and Peru.

Natural disasters

Following the 2010 Haiti earthquake, WCK established local kitchens and began distributing food. They returned to Haiti in the ensuing years, helping set up a cooking school in 2015.

Thereafter, in the United States, following Hurricane Harvey. And Puerto Rico, Bahamas, Australia, Turkey, Syria, Poland-Ukraine border, and Gaza.

In late February 2022, Andrés and WCK responded to multiple locations, including in border areas and in conflict zones such as hard-hit Kharkiv, Ukraine, to distribute meals during the 2022 Russian invasion. By March, WCK had opened eight kitchens on the Poland–Ukraine border.

In response to the ongoing humanitarian crisis, WCK has been contributing to food deliveries to the Gaza Strip.

The president of Cyprus had proposed a maritime humanitarian corridor for Gaza at a conference in Paris in early November 2023, and held talks the following month with the Egyptian president and Jordanian king. According to Cypriot authorities, there were also 'technical discussions' with Israeli officials. In an interview with Tel

Aviv Radio, the Israeli foreign minister said in December that 'it can start immediately'.

On 11 March, the ship was in Cyprus awaiting departure, after Cypriot authorities confirmed that permission had been granted. The goods were checked by Cypriot officials with Israeli oversight. It contained 'nearly 200 tons of food'.

By March 2024, WCK had provided more than 32 million meals.

The shipment arrived on 15 March at a beach south of Gaza City. According to WCK, this was the first boat to reach Gaza in nearly two decades.

Recognition

For his work with WCK, José Andrés won the 2018 James Beard Foundation Award for Humanitarian of the Year.

Andrés was named one of the world's 100 most influential people by *Time* magazine in 2018.

WCK won the 2021 Princess of Asturias Award.

WCK received a 2021 Courage and Civility Award from Jeff Bezos, along with a $100 million award.

In 2024, Andrés and WCK were nominated for the Nobel Peace Prize by former House Speaker Nancy Pelosi, and representatives Jim McGovern and Rosa DeLauro.

22nd August 2024

89 Amish

An Amish life for me

'καλόν δε και κόσμου λιτότης'

'Simplicity in adornment is finest'

- Democritus, 400 BCE

The Amish are a traditional Christian community that originated in Switzerland and headed westwards to the USA in the seventeenth and eighteenth centuries, settling first in Pennsylvania. Their way of life offers a counterbalance to the fast-paced, hyper-connected, and often anxious modern world. Their lifestyle is rooted in simplicity and tradition. The Amish population in the USA is around 400,000.

Simple minimalism

The Amish lifestyle is centred around simplicity, which is a stark contrast to the complexity and consumerism of modern society. Their emphasis on minimalism reduces the mental clutter and stress associated with unbridled consumerism, and our constant pursuit of material goods and social status. This simplicity fosters a life focused on essentials, leading to greater contentment and less anxiety.

Their dress code is humble; even buttons are considered ostentatious.

Strong community support

The Amish place a high value on community and family. In a world where people often feel isolated despite being digitally connected, the Amish experience strong interpersonal bonds, mutual support, and belonging. Their close-knit community offers emotional security and reduces the loneliness and anxiety that are common in modern society.

When someone needs to build a barn, everyone in the community gets involved and offers their skills. The men do the heavy lifting and the hammering. The women prepare food and drink, and look after the children.

Reduced digital overload

The Amish abstain from most modern technology, including the internet and smartphones, which are major sources of distraction, stress, and information overload. This avoids the constant bombardment of news, social media, and advertising, which contributes to anxiety and just being overwhelmed.

Manual labour

The Amish engage in manual labour, which keeps them physically active and connected to the land. This lifestyle contrasts with the sedentary habits common in modern life, where screen time dominates and physical activity is often neglected. Physical work not only keeps the body healthy but also provides a sense of accomplishment and purpose, especially when this is done in the service of others.

Spiritual fulfilment

The Amish lifestyle is deeply rooted in religious faith, which provides purpose and direction. In a world struggling with existential questions and a lack of meaning, the Amish find fulfilment through their faith, communal worship, and adherence to religious principles. This spiritual grounding helps them navigate life's challenges with peace and resilience.

Slow, intentional living

The Amish practice slow living, which emphasises intentionality and mindfulness in everyday activities. This approach allows them to savour the present moment and build deep connections with those around them. In contrast to the hurried pace of modern life, where people often rush from one task to the next, the Amish way of life encourages a more deliberate, thoughtful existence, reducing stress and promoting well-being.

Lifelong skills

The focus is on practical education and the acquisition of life skills rather than formal schooling. This hands-on learning and development prepares individuals to be competent and self-reliant. In a world where many feel disconnected from tangible achievements, the Amish lifestyle promotes competence and mastery over one's environment.

Preservation of cultural identity

The Amish maintain a strong cultural identity through their language, customs, and traditions. This continuity provides a powerful *rootedness,* stability and belonging, offering protection against the cultural fragmentation and identity crises that can arise in a rapidly changing world.

Amish life offers numerous advantages in an anxious world. By prioritising simplicity, community, modesty, manual labour, spiritual fulfilment, and independence, the Amish create a sustainable lifestyle that is more aligned with enduring human values.

27th August 2024

90 Amish II

Medical evidence

Clinical research evidence on the health outcomes, life expectancy, quality of life, and happiness among the Amish communities in North America, compared to the general population, reveals a number of key findings.

The Amish lifestyle is characterised by simplicity, physical activity, strong social support, and limited engagement with modern technology.

A traditional Christian community from Switzerland, the Amish settled in the USA over 200 years ago. The Amish population in the USA is around 400,000.

Health outcomes

Studies indicate that the Amish tend to have lower rates of many chronic conditions, such as heart disease, diabetes, and obesity, compared to the general population.

Their active lifestyle, which includes a lot of physical labour and a diet low in processed foods, contributes to this. They also tend to avoid smoking and excessive alcohol consumption, which further lowers their risk of these conditions.

Genetic conditions: Due to their relatively closed communities and higher rates of consanguinity (marriage between close relatives), the Amish experience higher incidences of certain genetic disorders, such as Ellis-van Creveld syndrome and certain metabolic disorders.

However, they have also developed strong community-based approaches to managing these conditions, often through specialised clinics and research collaborations.

Life expectancy

Comparable or slightly lower life expectancy: While the Amish may have lower rates of some chronic diseases, their life expectancy is generally comparable to or slightly lower than the general US population. This slight difference is often attributed to their higher rates of genetic disorders and their limited access to advanced medical interventions due to cultural or religious reasons.

Quality of Life

Despite their lower reliance on modern conveniences, the Amish report a high quality of life. Factors contributing to this include strong social support networks, a deep sense of community, low levels of stress related to materialism, and a focus on family and faith. Their slower-paced lifestyle and the value placed on manual work contribute to a sense of purpose and satisfaction.

The Amish appear to have lower rates of depression and anxiety than the general population. Their community-centric lifestyle, clear social roles, and strong religious faith offer protection against the mental health issues commonly associated with the stresses of modern life. However, mental health issues do exist in Amish communities, but they are often addressed within the community rather than through formal psychiatric services.

Happiness and well-being

The Amish consistently report high levels of happiness and life satisfaction. Their focus on spiritual and communal values over material success contributes to a sense of contentment. The emphasis on living a purposeful life, strong family bonds, and a supportive community environment likely play crucial roles in their overall well-being.

Other considerations

Due to their rural lifestyle, the Amish have less exposure to environmental pollutants and toxins, which may contribute to their overall health. Their use of homegrown food and minimal reliance on processed products also reduces their intake of harmful substances found in the modern diet.

While the Amish do seek medical care, they are less likely to use advanced medical technologies or interventions. Instead, they often rely on traditional remedies and community-based care. This can lead to better outcomes in some areas (e.g., fewer complications from medical interventions) but may result in worse outcomes in cases where advanced treatment is necessary.

Overall, the Amish experience relatively favourable health outcomes, high quality of life, and happiness levels due to their active lifestyle, strong community ties, and minimal exposure to modern stressors.

While they do face challenges related to genetic conditions and limited access to certain medical services, their lifestyle offers significant protective benefits against many of the chronic diseases and mental health issues prevalent in the general population. This suggests that their way of life, despite its simplicity, supports well-being in ways that many modern lifestyles do not.

30th December 2024

91 Baccalaureate

A new, local vision for education

Some visionary ideas for education are coming out of Manchester, aiming to transform the technical education in the city-region.

The Greater Manchester Baccalaureate, the MBacc, is set to grow the economy and help young people fulfil their potential.

Co-designed by education and business leaders, the MBacc will open up a clear pathway from school to high-quality jobs in the growing North West economy.

At present, only 40% of students in Greater Manchester study for an English Baccalaureate, a set of GCSE qualifications that are valued by universities. And a quarter achieve a standard pass in all subjects.

The MBacc has been designed as an equally-prestigious alternative for technical education, signposting young people to the subjects that Greater Manchester employers value most.

At 14, young people will be able to choose from seven MBacc gateways, designed with the help of some of prestigious employers and using local labour market data.

Qualifications are aligned to the sectors that are growing in Greater Manchester, namely: -

- Digital and Technology
- Health and Social Care
- Creative, Culture and Sport
- Financial and Professional
- Engineering and Manufacturing
- Construction and Green Economy
- Education and Early Years.

Young people will be prepared for the jobs of the future and digital skills will be hard-wired into the MBacc. Each gateway will be brought to life by real world experience of the workplace, including clear routes into the *Bee Network* (the integrated transport plan: named after the worker bee!) and emergency services.

The MBacc pathways continue post Year 11. At age 16, young people will have access to more technical (T level) courses than ever before, as well as other technical qualifications. A new central application system will open up work placements with employers.

Then at aged 18, MBacc students will have access to work-related courses, from intermediate and degree apprenticeships to higher technical qualifications.

The aim of the MBacc will be to help more young people to fulfil their potential, helping the Manchester metropolitan area achieve its goal of good lives for all.

The Mayor of Manchester, Andy Burnham, set out ten major points about the Manchester Baccalaureate, along with its goals and methods for achieving them.

1. Local Focus: tailored to the needs and strengths of Greater Manchester, aligning education with local economic and social priorities.
2. Broad Curriculum: emphasises a wide and balanced curriculum that includes both academic and vocational pathways, ensuring students develop a varied range of skills.
3. Work Readiness: a key component is preparing students for the workforce by emphasising employability skills, including teamwork, communication, and problem-solving.
4. Employer Engagement: local employers are directly involved in shaping the curriculum and providing work experience opportunities, ensuring the skills taught are relevant to the job market.
5. Accreditation: the Baccalaureate includes a form of accreditation that recognises students' achievements across a range of activities, not just traditional academic subjects.
6. Inclusion and Equity: ensuring that students from all backgrounds have access to high-quality education and opportunities.
7. Local Partnerships: schools, colleges, universities, and businesses in Greater Manchester work together to support the Baccalaureate, creating a cohesive education and employment ecosystem.
8. Real-World Learning: the curriculum includes real-world projects and practical experiences that help students apply their learning in meaningful ways.
9. Personal Development: a strong focus on the personal development of students, including their mental health and well-being.

10. Long-Term Vision: the Baccalaureate is part of a long-term vision for Greater Manchester's future, aiming to create a skilled, adaptable, and resilient workforce.

Goals

By providing students with relevant skills and experiences, the Baccalaureate aims to improve their job prospects and career readiness. And through aligning education with local economic needs, the initiative seeks to support economic growth and development in Greater Manchester.

The scheme aims to close the achievement gap and ensure that all students, regardless of their background, have access to high-quality education and opportunities. Overall the Baccalaureate aims to develop a skilled and adaptable workforce that can meet the demands of the local economy.

Through these strategies, the Manchester Baccalaureate aims to create a more relevant, inclusive, and effective education system that prepares students for the future.

3rd January 2025

Acknowledgements

Thank you to my wife Elena, and children, Nicholas and Neo, and to my wider family, relatives, friends, and work colleagues.

Thank you to The Estate of Seamus Heaney and *Faber & Faber*, for permission to use 'Sirens of the Tundra', from *Glanmore Sonnets, VII,* by Seamus Heaney.

And a huge thanks to my beloved students - past and present - from whom I learn so much.

References

Sources, by chapter

Introduction - *The Jewish Joke*, by Devorah Baum

3 - Parthenogenesis - *Parthenogenesis: Origins, Processes, and Outcomes,* by Warren Booth and Jack Werren, 2007; *The Evolution of Parthenogenesis,* by Johannes Breeuwer and Michael Stouthamer, 2000; *Reproduction Mode and the Evolution of Genome Architecture,* by John Avise and Jun Kitto, 2000; and *National Geographic* magazine.

5 - Winston - Andrew Roberts, *Triggernometry* podcast, 31st March 2024

15 - Sleep - Kat Lay, Health Editor, *The Times*

18 - Strangelove - *The Real Dr Strangelove,* by Peter Goodchild; *Prospect* magazine

24 - Dawn - Jason Kottke, 2018; Paolo Vivante, *Cambridge University Press*

27 - Spies - Katie Bo Lillis, *CNN*

28 - Tesla - Kristina Cooke and Dan Levine, *Reuters*

29 - Games - Hannah Fry on *Snowcast,* with John Snow, 23rd May 2023

31 - Airlines - *The Determinants of Airfares,* Volodymyr Bilotkach; and *Dynamic Pricing in the Airline Industry,* Michael Wittman and Roman Römisch

35 - Road - *The Rest is Politics* podcast, 25th October 2023

36 - Income - Brad Polumbo, *National Review,* 2023

38 - Teaching VII - Ethan Zuckerman, *Prospect* magazine, 2023

42 - Fibonacci II - *U.S. National Marine Sanctuary*

49 - One - *Power of One*, Jack Murtagh, *Scientific American*; Robert Matthews, *New Scientist*

50 - 85 - *The 85 Ways to Tie a Tie*, by Thomas Fink and Yong Mao, 1999

51 - Bloom - C-SPAN TV, and Charlie Rose

54 - Corridors - Matheus Gouvea de Andrade, *BBC Future,* 2023

58 - Kuwait III - *Lessons of Darkness,* directed by Werner Herzog, 1992

60 - Israel - Benny Morris, historian; Natasha Hausdorff, Barrister, *Six Pump Court Chambers*, Munk Debate, 2024

64 - North - Tom Whipple, Science Editor, *The Times*

67 - Now II - Douglas Murray, *The Free Press*

68 - Britain - *Institute for Global Change*: *Future of Britain* conference, July 2023

70 - Habits - *The Capitalist Manifesto,* Johan Norberg, 2023

73 - Fact - *Prospect* magazine

80 - Monkey - *Superfreakononics*, Steven Levitt and Stephen Dubner

81 - Names - Alexios Gennaris

84 - Fans - Kaya Burgess, *The Times*

86 - Philosemitism - *No Laughing Matter,* a conversation between Martin Amis and Christopher Hitchens, at *Jewish Book Week 2007,* hosted by *The Jewish Chronicle*

87 - Merry - Thank you to Alexandra Piha for introducing me to this story.

Wider references

The Free Press, Racket News by Matt Taibbi, Financial Times, The Times, i-Paper, Reuters, Honestly with Bari Weiss, The New Yorker, Bloomberg, NPR, Institute of Economic Affairs, The Lex Fridman podcast, The Reading Rooms and the Members Room of the British Library, and The Marginalian.

Any copyright infringement is unintended. Every endeavour has been made to credit the relevant sources. Any plagiarism in this book is inadvertent, innocent of any intent, and the result of sloth. All remaining errors are the author's. The publishers will rectify any misappropriation, or cite any unattributed sources, in any future editions.

'Index'

Most common words or people in this book / Number of mentions

Music....82
Work....72
Israel....58
Mathematics....57
Tradition / traditional....55
Women / female....47
U.S.A. / US....43
Language....38
Sleep....38
Money....34
Men / male....31
Civilisation / civil / civilian / civic....29
Food....27
Homer....26
Greece....25
London....24
UK....23
Books....21
Cyprus....17

www.ingramcontent.com/pod-product-compliance
Lightning Source LLC
Chambersburg PA
CBHW030553170726
48283CB00002B/298